A
HISTORY OF
EVERYDAY THINGS
IN ENGLAND

A street scene: an organ grinder
Painting by L. S. Lowry

A
HISTORY OF
EVERYDAY THINGS
IN ENGLAND

Volume V
1914–1968

S. E. ELLACOTT

Foreword by PETER QUENNELL

B. T. BATSFORD LTD LONDON

First Impression 1968
Second Impression 1970
Third Impression 1977
Fourth Impression 1980

©S. E. Ellacott 1968
© Foreword Peter Quennell 1968
ISBN 0 7134 1654 8

01146459

ACKNOWLEDGMENT

THE author and publishers would like to thank the following for permission to reproduce the illustrations in this book: Radio Times Hulton Picture Library for Figs. 13, 16, 17, 27, 30, 41, 48, 51, 55, 56, 57, 65, 67, 68, 70, 75, 80, 99; Paul Popper Ltd (Popperfoto) for Figs. 5, 64, 69, 78, 79; Keystone Press Agency Ltd for Figs. 18, 71; *Farmers Weekly* for Fig. 50; Fox Photos Ltd for Fig. 63; Colston Appliances Ltd for Fig. 12; I.B.M. for Fig. 58; Mirropic for Fig. 35; British Hovercraft Corporation for Fig. 106; Rank Organisation for Fig. 42; Manchester City Art Gallery for the frontispiece; Mr R. A. S. Hennessey for the table on pages 8 and 9.

BLACKPOOL DISTRICT

BP	BA		
	3	86		

MADE AND PRINTED IN GREAT BRITAIN BY BUTLER & TANNER LTD
FROME AND LONDON FOR THE PUBLISHERS
B. T. BATSFORD LTD
4 Fitzhardinge Street, London W1H 0AH

CONTENTS

LIST OF ILLUSTRATIONS

The numerals in parentheses in the text refer to the *figure numbers* of the illustrations

Frontispiece: A street scene: an organ grinder by L. S. Lowry

LIST OF ILLUSTRATIONS

Political	Social
1914 (to 1918) First World War	1914 Agriculture—minimum wage 19s. per wee[k]
1915 Britain blockaded	Stringent liquor law: modern licensing bo[urs]
Lusitania sunk	
Gallipoli	
Rent control	
1916 Easter Rebellion, Dublin	
Lloyd George Prime Minister	
1917 All-out U-boat war	
1918 Coupon Election	
Votes for women	
1919 Amritsar Massacre	
1922 Geddes 'Axe'	1922 B.B.C. formed
Fall of Lloyd George	
Irish Free State	1923 First Wembley Cup Final
1924 First Labour Government	
First woman M.P.	
'Wheatley' Housing Act	
	1927 Last volume of Havelock Ellis' *Psycholog[y]*
	Sex
	1928 Death of Thomas Hardy
	1930 Death of Conan Doyle
1931 National Government	Housing Act, to clear slums
1932 Import Duties Act: end of 'free trade'	1932 Town and Country Planning Act
1933 Hitler Chancellor of Germany	
1934 Peace ballot	
Unemployment Act	1935 Chanel 'cardigan suit'—hardy perennial
1936 EDWARD VIII	1936 Deaths of G. K. Chesterton and Rud[yard]
Abdication	Kipling
	B.B.C. TV. starts
1937 GEORGE VI	Jarrow March
1938 Munich crisis	1938 *Picture Post* launched
1939 (to 1945) Second World War	1939 Death of Yeats
1940 Battle of Britain	1940 Barlow Report
Bombing of major cities	1941 Clothes rationing
Winston Churchill P.M.	1942 Beveridge Report
Dunkirk	Soap rationing
1944 Flying bombs	1944 Education Act (Butler)
	Full Employment in a Free Society (Bever[idge])
1945 Atomic bombs dropped on Japan	1945 Family allowances
Labour Government	1946 New Towns Act
Nationalisation of: Bank of England 1946	National Insurance Act
Coal 1947	National Health Service Act (operative
Railways and Electricity	1948)
1948	
Gas 1949	
Iron and Steel 1951 and	
1967	
1947 End of Britain's Indian Empire	1947 Town and Country Planning Act
Marshall Plan launched	TV. restarts after war
	Dior's 'New Look'
1948 Representation of the People Act: 'one man,	1948 National Assistance Act
one vote'	
1949 £1 devalued (first)	1949 End of clothes rationing
	1950 Death of G. B. Shaw
	1951 Festival of Britain
1953 ELIZABETH II	
	1954 Independent TV. authorised
1955 Winston Churchill retires, Anthony Eden P.M.	1955 End of meat rationing
1956 Suez crisis	
1957 Anthony Eden retires, Harold Macmillan P.M.	1957 Consumers' Association
	1958 J. K. Galbraith: *Affluent Society*
1960 Death of Aneurin Bevan	
E.F.T.A. formed	
1963 Profumo scandal	1963 Worst winter for 200 years
	Bishop of Woolwich: *Honest To God*
	Newsom Report
1964 Labour Government, Harold Wilson P.M.	1964 H.P. debt passes £1,000 million
1965 Death of Sir Winston Churchill	
1967 £1 devalued (second)	1967 10 million cars on the roads
	1968 Death of Sir Harold Nicolson
	£1 worth 3s 5d. at 1914 prices

Science and Industry		The Arts
	1911	Diaghilev's Ballets Russes in Britain
5 Gas warfare and aerial bombing	1915	Holst: *The Planets*
	1916	*Chu Chin Chow*—runs for five years
	1917	Bax: *Tintagel*
		Epstein: *Venus*
		Paul Nash official war artist
8 'Big Five' banks	1918	Sickert: *Pulteney Bridge*
9 Alcock and Brown fly Atlantic	1919	Jazz arrives in Britain
0 Electricity Supply Act		
Medical Research Council		
1 2 million unemployed		
2 Insulin	1922	Somerset Maugham: *East of Suez*
Austin 7 car		T. S. Eliot: *Waste Land*
First King's Cup Air Race		James Joyce: *Ulysses*
3 Railways grouped	1923	Shaw: *St Joan*
4 Wembley Exhibition		First super cinema
National electricity grid built	1926	The Charleston
General Strike		T. E. Lawrence: *Seven Pillars of Wisdom*
Television invented by J. L. Baird		Lutyens: Britannic House
	1927	Virginia Woolf: *To The Lighthouse*
Bank of England issues £1 and 10s. notes	1928	Cinematograph Act
First 'airport' (Croydon)		Noel Coward: *This Year of Grace*
Beginning of discovery of penicillin		Evelyn Waugh: *Decline and Fall*
		D. H. Lawrence: *Lady Chatterley's Lover*
	1929	Robert Bridges: *Testament of Beauty*
Nylon		Noel Coward: *Bitter Sweet*
R101 disaster		J. B. Priestley: *The Good Companions*
Road Traffic Act		Robert Graves: *Good-bye to All That*
Depth of the 'Slump'	1932	Aldous Huxley: *Brave New World*
Cockcroft, Rutherford *et al.* 'split the atom'		H. G. Wells (film): *The Shape of Things to Come*
S.R. London–Brighton line electrified	1933	Korda: *The Private Life of Henry VIII* (with Charles Laughton)
Radar (Watson–Watt)	1935	Mendelssohn and Chermayeff: De La Warr Pavilion, Bexhill
		Vaughan Williams: Fourth Symphony
Keynes' *General Theory*	1936	Kensal House Housing Scheme (Fry)
World steam speed record: L.N.E.R. 'Mallard'		
Colour TV.		
Jet engine (Whittle)		
	1942	Death of Walter Sickert
	1945	*The Seventh Veil*
Fuel crisis		
Agriculture Act		
	1948	*The Red Shoes*
Manchester University 'Mechanical Brain'	1949	Orwell: *Nineteen Eighty-four*
Cortisone		
Terylene		
'Brabazon' giant aeroplane	1951	Festival of Britain: Dome of Discovery and Skylon
Last London tram		
Comet 1 jet airliner	1953	Henry Moore: *King and Queen*
	1954	Kingsley Amis: *Lucky Jim*
First Atomic-powered generating station (Calder Hall)	1956	Spa Green Flats (Tecton)
Jodrell Bank radio telescope		Osborne: *Look Back in Anger*
Royal Greenwich Observatory completes move to Herstmonceux		
Cross-Channel electric power link		
Motorway plan		
U.S.A.–Europe TV. link	1962	Coventry Cathedral, *designed* by Spence
		windows by Piper
Ministry of Technology		*tapestry* by Sutherland
Natural gas under North Sea		*sculpture* by Epstein
Hovercraft in operation		
Tay and Severn bridges opened		
British heart transplant		
Jodrell Bank probes 'the very limits of the Universe'		

FOREWORD

by Peter Quennell

MY father was born on 5 June 1872, the eldest son of Henry Quennell, a somewhat unsuccessful builder, and his wife Emma Bourne, who, before her marriage, had been the energetic proprietor and director of a small private school near London. My grandfather's habits were feckless: he was an easy-going, good-natured person, who much preferred playing or watching cricket to building houses in the suburbs; and my father's childhood was overshadowed by the constant threat of poverty. As a middle-aged man, I remember, he told me that, although he appreciated the genius of Charles Dickens, he could not bear to read the famous novels, since their detailed pictures of shabby-genteel life—of 'little grey people in little grey streets': such was the expressive phrase he used at the time—reminded him far too vividly of his own youth.

Thus he was attached to his father, but had a deep admiration, which never failed, for his possessive and autocratic mother; it was she who, at a particularly low ebb in their fortunes, had prevented her husband from sending his children to a nearby council school. She was proud of her eldest son. My father had inherited something of her vigorous spirit; and, having received a respectable schooling and adopted the profession of architecture, he soon began to make his way. Unlike my grandfather, he had a passion for hard work; but he, too, loved the open air and had a cheerful and gregarious nature. He was fond of waltzing and, with his broad shoulders and tall slender frame, looked, I am told, extremely well upon the dance-floor. He was also a good horseman; and, when he was a young man, he spent many holidays riding to hounds across the moors of Somerset.

Then, in the year 1904, he met and married my mother Marjorie Courtney. It was an extraordinarily happy alliance; but, once he had embarked on married life, my father gave up all his youthful pleasures. Henceforward he neither danced nor hunted, and devoted his entire existence to his profession and his family.

By 1912 he had been elected a member of the Council of the Royal Institute of British Architects, and had earned the reputation among his professional colleagues of being a notably ingenious planner. Hundreds of the trim, compact houses that he designed can still be recognised around London. As his own home, at Bickley, on the urban fringes of Kent, he had built a house he called 'Four Beeches', after a group of old trees that he had incorporated in its large and pleasant garden—a dignified neo-Georgian building, where he continued to live until the beginning of the First World War.

That disaster transformed his whole career; the demand for middle-sized modern houses, in which he had hitherto specialised, was abruptly cut short; and, from being a prosperous executant, he became a comparatively poor man, obliged to earn a small living by means of uncongenial war-work. Had Europe escaped the tragedy, my father's life might have taken a very different, possibly a happier and smoother, but certainly a much less interesting turn. His last commission, undertaken just before the outbreak of hostilities, was the largest and most profitable he had yet obtained; and no doubt he would have gone on steadily improving his position and adding to his yearly income. As it was, confronting Dickensian poverty, among the horrors and discomforts of a world at war, he revived a long-suppressed ambition. He decided that he would write a book; and the idea of producing a new type of social history, written from the intelligent layman's point of view, gradually materialised.

He had little previous experience of writing; though in 1900 he had published a study of Norwich Cathedral and, in 1906, an illustrated volume, entitled *Modern Suburban Houses*; nor could he ever have been called a literary man. But he had ideas, a keen desire to express them and not the smallest touch of false pride; and, once he conceived the notion of writing a book, he forged ahead by a process of trial and error. The result appeared in the autumn of 1918. That autumn there was a dearth of new titles; and, more important, the British reading public, sickened by the long drama of wartime death and destruction, welcomed a book that appealed, repeatedly and forcefully, to mankind's most constructive instincts; that described the splendid achievements of the past, and sought to apply the lessons we could learn from the past to the problems of the present day.

11

It was a scheme, I think, that would have delighted both John Ruskin and his Pre-Raphaelite follower William Morris. Here again was Ruskin's Gospel of Work, accompanied by the suggestion that good workmanship played a decisive part in the creation of aesthetic beauty. My father, however, was no aesthete—he had learned to dread the name of Oscar Wilde; and, although some of his early designs for furniture show a certain Art Nouveau influence, he modelled his artistic standards on the austere example of the Middle Ages. There he felt at home and at peace. Some of the happiest hours of his life were passed visiting and drawing village churches, examining the remains of a painted rood-screen or investigating the mysteries of the so-called 'Leper's Squint'.

The first volume of *A History of Everyday Things in England* covered the period 1066 to 1453. My father was not quite so much at ease with the Renaissance, which had a tinge of worldly paganism; but he always admired, wherever he found it, really sound constructive work; and, as the project increased its scope, he rapidly enlarged his views, until even the Industrial Age began, in some respects, to gain his sympathy. Granted the limitations of his private moral code—his ethical beliefs were those of his late Victorian youth—he had a wonderfully sympathetic and receptive mind.

It might be unjust to say that my father definitely preferred things to people; but it is true that he always regarded things—if rightly designed and capably executed—as a distillation of people's finest feelings; and that he was apt to dismiss emotion, and the strange vagaries of human conduct, as an unnecessary waste of time. His hero was the Craftsman—the dedicated individual, who, disregarding personal sentiment, went straight ahead and 'got things done'. The theme of craftsmanship runs through all his books; for he remembered a day when rural England was still populated by highly skilled workers; and during his youth, after a serious illness, he had spent some time in a secluded Kentish village, where he had made friends with the local carpenter and had learned the woodworking trade at his old-fashioned bench.

The world war had finally destroyed his vision of self-reliant rustic England; the thatchers, wheelwrights, carpenters and blacksmiths were disappearing from the country; and today it was an oil-spattered mechanic bestriding a tractor, not a corduroyed ploughman with a noble team of horses, who drove a ploughshare through the fields. But my father hoped that the spirit of the old England could be restored to meet the new conditions. Whatever men built, they must learn to build well; and whatever they planned must be planned soundly, soberly and honestly. He himself had discovered his real vocation; and to that vocation, though, now and then, he still practised as an architect, he consecrated his remaining years.

During the 1920s he built a second home—much smaller and less comfortable than the first—just above the Hertfordshire town of Berkhamsted; and it was there that I watched him year by year adding volumes to his project. He had my mother's loyal cooperation. Possibly because it was less expensive, we did not yet employ electric lighting. We relied on gas; and some of my parents' early work was done under the uncertain glow of a fluttering, greenish gas-mantle. Their desks stood side by side; and my father, having completed his re-creation of a thirteenth-century castle or fifteenth-century manor-house, would promptly hand it to my mother, suggesting that she should enliven the foreground with interesting human shapes. Why not a knight and a lady, a page holding a horse, perhaps a little boy and an attractive dog? He had left a series of oblong apertures, vertical or horizontal, large and small, which my devoted mother then filled in.

Her province was the study of costume and armour; my father concentrated his attention on architecture and mechanical devices. My father could not manage figures; my mother could not draw buildings. Perspective, not my mother's forte, was among my father's strongest suits; and every one of the full-page illustrations was based on a complex preliminary framework of converging pencil-lines. It was in small illustrations that my mother excelled. These vignettes, which represented, for instance, 'A Judicial Combat', 'A Game with Soldiers', 'A Baker of Short-weight Loaves being drawn to the Pillory', 'A Bird-cage Seller' or 'A Performing Bear', displayed her talent at its happiest. The slightly stylised character of her draughtsmanship tended to increase the drawing's charm; but at the time, I sometimes teased her about her personages' formal airs and graces, and what I impertinently called their 'Anglo-Saxon attitudes'.

Writing *Everyday Things in England*, and the numerous volumes that succeeded it, was an agreeably domestic business. My parents' joint studio was the family sitting room; for the house we now

13

occupied was by no means large; and my father liked to read and work among his children, provided, of course, that they were not too noisy; though, as a rule, he objected to noise—even to the cacophonous hubbub of an early radio—much less than many other artists. During the earlier stages of the project, he very often worked at night. I remember the gas-lit and fire-lit room, the smell of Indian ink and tracing paper, the sheets of Bristol board on the adjacent desks and the harsh whisper of a scratching pen. Stout reference books were heaped on shelves and tables—Viollet-le-Duc, Traill's *Social History* and Nash's *Homes of Other Days.*

Ordinariness was a quality that my father valued; and it was from the point of view of an 'ordinary, decent' man—both adjectives he used as terms of high praise—that he endeavoured to approach his subject. He was not an ordinary man himself; but he had conceived a profound respect for the least complicated human virtues; and those were the virtues he had in mind when he came to write history. He did not write primarily for adults; 'boys and girls of public school age' were the audience at which he aimed; they, as he explained in his introduction, might hope to build a brave new England:

> Boys and girls who are now growing up will be given opportunities that no other generation has ever had; and it is of the greatest importance that they should be trained to do useful work and learn to use their hands. Before they can become actual constructors and craftsmen, able and worthy to carry on the work of the world, they must obtain a good store of knowledge—lay hold of tradition, so that they can benefit by what has been done—know that in one direction progress can be made, and that in another it will be arrested. Thus the coming generation may combine the wonderful appreciation for the uses and beauty of material that the old craftsmen possessed, with the opportunities for production which the modern machine gives, and so launch a new era of beautiful everyday things.

As we know, when his books appeared, they were bought and enjoyed, not only by boys and girls, but by an immense variety of grown-up readers. The opening volume of *Everyday Things* had an immediate success in 1918; and none of the books with which he followed it—apart from a single volume, written at the very end of his life—has subsequently gone out of print. Before he died in 1935, besides providing three further volumes of the original *Everyday Things*, which carried on the narrative until the outbreak of the First World War, he had covered *Everyday Life in Pre-historic Times*, *Everyday Life in Roman and Anglo-Saxon Times* and the life of Homeric, Archaic and Classical Greece.

Each was the product of a new enthusiasm—my father, as I have tried to show, had a passionately enthusiastic spirit; and, no sooner had he begun a book, than he became deeply immersed in its historical background. He loved the mediaeval period, but plunged with equal relish into a study of prehistoric Europe. Then at home we heard of nothing but Piltdown Man—who had not yet fallen from archaeological favour—eoliths, cave-paintings, primitive tools and weapons, and the movements of the polar ice-cap that had sent gigantic glaciers crawling down the globe. Over a family meal he would set out to explain the process, and with the help of an orange, transfixed by a knitting needle, demonstrate exactly what had happened.

If my father was a born enthusiast, he was also an inveterate optimist. True, in his domestic circle, he often struck a gloomy note, and would talk of his own early death—here, alas, his predictions were justified: when he succumbed to a slowly exhausting illness, he was only sixty-three—and of the 'work-house' that, unless we could somehow reduce our expenses, certainly loomed straight ahead. But his view of the world at large was cheerful; and he found an unfailing source of pleasure in the contemplation of its artefacts. There he discovered the reassurance he sought; and being fundamentally an anxious man—his childhood had implanted a strain of anxiety that he could never wholly overcome —he always wanted reassurance. The fine construction of a medieval water-mill or an early nineteenth-century windmill, of a farm wagon, a plough or an adze, a Gothic vault or a timber-framed roof, revealed that, despite war and politics, the ordinary, decent man need not despair.

It is not easy to describe a character that included so many diverse traits. But almost all of them are reflected in the books that today provide his most enduring monument. My father's writings were rarely impersonal; the personal touch was perpetually creeping in; and, though here and there some private hobby or fad—for example, his concern with the mechanics of sanitation: he had made an intensive study of ancient *garderobes*—threatened to develop into a King Charles' Head, on the whole it had a salutary effect. My father seems to be inviting his audience to accompany him in his adventures, and to share his own discoveries. His prose has a freshness and verve—a kind of enthusiastic bounce or spring —that seldom distinguishes works of social history.

Everyday Things in England, Volume I, was first published 50 years ago. It has had numerous imitators; but none of the authors who followed its lead has disposed of quite the same advantages. My mother and father were a closely united team; each contributed qualities that the other lacked; and their joint productions have all the light-and-shade of their varying, and sometimes, opposing interests. To celebrate the anniversary of *Everyday Things*, Mr S. E. Ellacott has ably rounded off the series. His subject is the twentieth century and the organisation of the post-war world. Would my father have enjoyed living—he would now have been 96—in the year 1968? Some aspects of the modern age—its ugliness, its growing urbanisation and its permissive sexual ethics—would certainly have horrified him. Elsewhere, I feel sure, he would have found much to praise. I have no doubt that he would have admired the Welfare State. He had long detested poverty and injustice; and, as I have said before, he was by temperament a profoundly hopeful man.

Chapter I

THE HOME

IN 1914 England was only four years removed from the Edwardian era, associated with 'class distinction' in housing—stately home and revolting slum, pillared portico and broken doorstep. This is an oversimplification, but in 1914 housing conditions had been virtually static for at least 20 years.

A 'great house' in a town was organised along the same hierarchical lines as before, with dining and drawing rooms on the ground floor, and family bedrooms above. By 1914 bathrooms were common in great houses. Under the roof in the garrets were the servants' quarters, and below ground were the kitchen, larder, servery, and wash-house. There was the same overabundance of carved ornament and furniture, which collected dust easily, and the same hard-labour cleaning and polishing apparatus.

It is true that dusting and carpet-cleaning were mechanically aided by the use of hand-worked vacuum cleaners(1). These were first employed about 1908; a rotary brush, like that of a carpet-sweeper, brought up the dust for suction. As the drawing shows, a bellows action performed the dust intake, while in the earlier models the dust-laden air was filtered through a water-chamber. Electric vacuum cleaners became quite well known by 1917, but their use was limited to progressive households, as human cleaners were cheap and plentiful.

Large town houses had the advantage of being individual. Such houses were seldom to be found in rows, but in closely built-up town areas there was the painful sight of identical terraced houses in a grid-iron of successive lines. An example of such building may be seen to this day in some parts of Southsea, the Portsmouth resort town. Its worst form was created in the great factory towns, with their notorious back-to-back dwellings. A variation of this crammed housing was the tunnel-back arrangement, where a dark, foul passage lay between the backs, bridged over by the opposing upper storey.

This was the darkest side of the communal picture, but one or two far-sighted factory owners' combines were pioneers of model communities for workers, as shown in Volume IV of this series. For more than 15 years, the only example of Ebenezer Howard's suggested garden cities was Letchworth. That flourishing community in North Hertfordshire, 47 miles from London, was founded in 1903. It was built on a concentric system, with a park, and shops at the centre. This example led a few enterprising builders to create low-density dwelling areas, at the rate of 12 houses to the acre. When cheaper travel facilities encouraged some workers to live on the outskirts of their towns, central congestion was eased and suburbs developed.

1 Bellows-type vacuum cleaner, 1908

In the country, appearances were deceptive. A labourer's cottage presented a pleasing aspect, set in its old-world garden, with roses around the cottage door. But despite its picturesqueness the cottage had many disadvantages. That old thatched roof, beloved of the artist and charmingly mellowed, harboured rats and fleas; it was a grave fire risk, and it was hard to repair a small section without wholesale rethatching.

An inside arrangement of two rooms up and two down was common, the ground floor comprising a living room-cum-kitchen and a back kitchen (2). If the walls were of cob—a mixture of clay, straw, horsehair, and small pebbles—as was often the case, there was a choice of two interior finishes. One might whitewash the walls, which would give the appearance of a barn, or hang wallpaper. When the latter was used, an incautious knock against the wall might bring down a rattling shower of loose cob inside the paper, which thus became a bag of crumbled rubble.

At the top of the steep, narrow stairs were the bedrooms, possibly with no ceiling. This gave a delightful mediaeval effect, but during the night pieces of detached material might flutter

2   Devonshire workman's cottage, 1914

down upon upturned faces, and on a windy night the draughts were considerable. Where a ceiling did exist, the sleeper below might be disturbed by nightly rat-races overhead. Other enemies to comfort were the small windows and dim interior, the bucket water supply, and the outside earth closet. Lighting was mainly by the paraffin lamp, supported by candles; the kettle was the only source of hot water, daily washing was done at a bowl, and a bath was a major operation.

Even in the third quarter of the twentieth century, such conditions are not entirely unknown: insanitary cottages and slum dwellings still exist. Indeed, there has been a long, hard struggle in the cause of better housing since John Burns, President of the Local Government Board, introduced the first Housing and Town Planning Act in 1909. It was designed to deal with two main needs: rented houses were necessary for the lower-income worker, while the rising lower middle class and the skilled men were seeking house ownership.

In spite of good intentions, the outbreak of war in 1914 stifled what little progress had been made in house-building and slum clearance. Of course, there was no building during the war years. In fact, Government attention was drawn to existing rented houses with unscrupulous landlords, who, finding their costs increasing, began to raise their rents unreasonably. It was an intolerable position for soldiers' wives on allowance, for instance; with a low income, dear food, and increased rent they were sometimes reduced to starvation level. By means of the Rent and Mortgage Restriction Act of 1915, the Government provided against house shortage and the possible eviction of tenants.

When the war was over, the authorities were faced with the need for cheap houses, to be erected quickly and in large numbers. Two great drawbacks for would-be contractors were high building costs and high interest rates for intending borrowers on mortgage. Private builders could not afford to produce houses to rent while they were restricted by the Rent Act; yet if rents were freed, an excessive increase might follow.

This problem was tackled when Viscount Addison, Minister of Reconstruction, brought in the Housing and Town Planning Act (1919), which made all local authorities responsible for dealing with housing in their own areas. A penny rate was fixed to

3   Housing styles after 1918. (*Top*) Welwyn Garden City, 1920. (*Bottom*) Survival of traditional style at Ashley Close, Dorset, 1929

help with costs, and the remainder was provided by a Government subsidy. Under this scheme, 176,000 houses of fairly good standard were built. Though the subsidies were withdrawn after two years, further help was arranged in 1923 and 1924.

One of the rules covering the second subsidy grant was that private builders had to work within limits. In order to gain grants, a two-storey house had to cover an area of between 620 and 950 square feet, while for a bungalow or flat the figures were 550 and 880. It was also laid down that each dwelling should have a fixed bath, which, under the 1924 rules, had to be in a bathroom.

This was the beginning of the bungalow era and of the blocks of flats that have become such a familiar sight. Until 1927, flat-dwellers under London County Council often shared baths. Even at that date, there were efforts to provide clothes-drying space, pram sheds, separate balconies, clubrooms, and play areas for flat-dwellers.

Thus, in the space of only eight years, official provision and direction of dwelling-places was in full swing—an unheard-of social experiment.

Having begun to provide for construction, the Government then turned its attention to destruction. Every town of any size in England had a number of low-class houses known as 'slum property'. 'Slum' is an expressive slang word of uncertain origin. It conveys a mental picture of dirty, decrepit houses crowded in befouled streets, with inhabitants to match.

In 1929 the National Housing and Town Planning Council suggested a scheme for solving the problem, and a year later a housing Act (Greenwood's Slum Clearance Act) came into force. Landlords who moved tenants from slum property were subsidised at a fixed rate for every family rehoused. Shortly after this move came the Town and Country Planning Act of 1932, the purpose of which was to prevent the haphazard siting of houses and the needless destruction of amenities, as well as to preserve agricultural land.

By that time (1932) nearly a quarter of a million houses had been built, just under half by local authorities on subsidies and most of the rest by private builders helped in the same way. In spite of this achievement, remarkable for that period, prices were fairly high. A medium-size town house, in a good district, cost £1,000, a new terrace house about £500, and a detached bungalow

£600, while the mortgage rate was five per cent. This was at a time when a tradesman's pay was about £3 a week.

Human nature being what it is, the building boom gave opportunity for cheating, and the term 'jerry builder' became familiar. It was applied to a builder who used shoddy materials and short-cut methods.

There arose from all these activities a social problem that was peculiar to the times. With the rehousing of former slum-dwellers on council-built estates, many tenants appeared to feel the change very keenly. No doubt many of the tales about their conduct originated among the disgruntled owners of private houses in the areas chosen for estates. However, such oddities as the keeping of coal and pigeons in the bath kept recurring, so possibly some of the tenants did misuse their new homes. On the other hand, official efforts to keep down the cost led to such features as a bathroom so narrow that the bath could only be entered by climbing over the end. In one kind of West Country municipal house, the bath was sunk into the floor under the kitchen table.

This was the beginning of the great age of concrete, a material which largely superseded the traditional brick, stone, and cob of past centuries. Yet concrete itself is a substance of ancient origin. There are examples of Roman concrete still in existence. Concrete is basically cement, which is made by burning together some form of lime and clay. Portland cement is used in building; it was so called by its inventor, Joseph Aspdin, the Yorkshire bricklayer who produced the cement in 1824, because in its hard state it looked like Portland stone.

When cement is used for concrete, it is mixed with sand and gravel, and the chief use is in 'cast' form—as foundations, and for roads, posts, pillars and lintels, building blocks, etc. Reinforced concrete is cast upon steel rods of up to two inches diameter. This was first used in buildings in the 1890s, by François Hennebique in France and Frederick Ransome in America.

Concrete building blocks were not commonly employed for outside house walls until about 1930, but they were used for the 'inner skin' of the double or cavity wall of the twentieth-century house. This form of wall has a space between the 'skins' to provide insulation against damp. After a few courses of bricks or blocks have been laid on the foundations, a broad strip of lead is laid round the outside wall, to check rising damp. Old-time builders of cob walls laid about 18 inches of stonework as a 'damp course' before beginning the cob.

By 1955, outside walls of concrete blocks were often used for houses, and usually the inner skin was of 'breeze' blocks. These were made of crushed coke, with a little cement for bonding, and they formed a useful material for partition walls.

Though the building of council houses was not very profitable, because the price was restricted, many builders accepted the work to keep their men going when other contracts were scarce. Throughout the 1920s, building was maintained at a fairly high rate, but the slump years 1929–32 brought unemployment to the industry. In spite of Government reviews of the subsidy, building declined during that difficult period. However, there was a revival by 1935, for in that year an Act restricting ribbon development became law. This meant that builders could not line a highway with houses giving a straggling effect.

Amid the owner-occupier building drive, there were still many thousands of families in rented houses; the great era of house purchase had not then begun. Government attention was drawn to the rent question, another feature of the domestic revolution. Before 1914, rent was arranged by agreement between landlord and tenant, with no outside influence, just as, until 1919, house-building was a matter between buyer and builder. Rent restriction by authority, first brought in as a wartime measure, became a permanent feature of property law.

Between 1920 and 1939 a number of Acts dealt with the tenancy of all but the most costly houses. In London, the tenant of an unfurnished house with a rateable value of not more than £100 could not be forced to leave it. Even if the tenant broke the agreement, the landlord had to get a court order to evict him. The occupier could not be evicted at the end of the agreed period of tenancy unless the terms of the agreement contravened the Rent Act. There were similar regulations to cover houses of up to £75 rateable value situated outside London.

Of course, these laws made it hard to find unfurnished houses to rent. If such a house became vacant, the rent could not be raised by more than 10 per cent, in spite of repair costs, so the landlord would probably let it 'furnished'. As long as the bare essentials were in the house, it was classed in that way, with no rent restriction and such terms as the landlord chose.

4 'Prefabs', Oakleigh Road, Barnstaple

During the war years 1939–45 there was little progress in building, and the great towns suffered widespread damage. Many families were sent from the target areas to safer parts of the country. These 'evacuees' were housed in requisitioned property, or billeted upon households with spare rooms. Troops were sometimes billeted in the same manner.

At the end of the war, there was a shortage of roughly a million houses through bomb damage, so emergency schemes were needed. One of the first concerned rent, for landlords with furnished property were inclined to make up their wartime losses by raising rents. This was quickly settled by the Furnished Houses (Rent Control) Act of 1946, which allowed a tenant to apply to a rent tribunal for a reduction of rent.

Building by local authorities was permitted under control, each district being allocated permits for a certain number of houses to rent. This gave rise to many problems; a list of applicants was considered on a system of points, i.e. urgency or deserving condition. All building materials were short, especially seasoned timber, so private building could only be done under licence. In this case the licence was issued by the Central Land Board as a permit to buy enough timber. Emergency council schemes included the mass production of prefabricated houses in asbestos sheeting(4); the double walls were packed with insulating material. These 'prefabs' were strange-looking, square, flat-topped boxes, but they were surprisingly roomy and comfortable.

Further control on building came with the Town and Country Planning Act of 1947. Under this Act, any form of building needed 'planning permission', in case any objection was raised. If permission was obtained, the Central Land Board assessed the site for its 'development value', and a fee had to be paid.

In most cases alterations to existing property required planning permission, and owners who began building or altering houses without authority were ordered to destroy their work. Other restrictions on 'developers' were the size, shape, colour, and angle of the proposed building in relation to its surroundings. Planning authorities usually arranged a 'green belt' around built-up areas to preserve the countryside, but a good deal of encroachment took place. If a large-scale building scheme was being carried out by a local council, property obstructing its progress could be taken over by 'compulsory purchase' if the owner would not sell. Often, a very low figure was paid for the property.

Government grants were given, under the Housing Act of 1949, in cases where a big house was divided into flats. A grant of up to £800 was allowed for converting a barn into a dwelling-house, and an owner wishing to install a bathroom in his house was granted £100. At about the same time there was an increase in the number of 'temporary' dwellings. These were made of perforated steel plating called 'expanded metal', timber, asbestos, and wall-boarding with plaster. Temporary buildings cost about £500 as against the current price of £1,800 for a brick bungalow. A number of temporary buildings exist in good repair, but in the early 1950s the Law Society forbade solicitors to arrange mortgages on such houses, as being insufficient security for loans.

Permanent houses and bungalows of that period showed a number of typical mid-twentieth-century features. Steel window-frames had been in general use for some years, as the old-type wooden sash was prone to mishap and jamming. Though steel frames were strong and warp-free, they were subject to unsightly rust unless painting was regularly carried out. There were two main types of roofing—asbestos slates and concrete tiles, in a choice of several colours. If the latter were used, the total weight was several tons, so roof timbers had to be reliable. Builders had almost abandoned the old-style quarried slate, which was apt to break.

An increasing amount of attention to window-space meant more interior light as well as a freer view of the exterior. By 1955 the picture-window was very popular—a large expanse of glass without crossing bars, the casement being at the side. This was a characteristic of the elegant houses of Cubitt, and the long line of linked lights was a feature of Eric Lyons' graceful designs for tile-hung dwellings. Probably the greatest postwar architect was the famous French designer Le Corbusier (Charles Edouard Jeaunaret, 1887–1965). Most of his work was done on the Continent, but it had great influence on housing sites in the London area.

On sites with a gentle slope, the split-level dwelling was often seen, where roof and floor showed a step. Bungalows were much favoured in the country and the suburbs, with the variation of the semi-bungalow which had a room in the roof. Where great bomb damage had been done in the large centres, the sites were cleared and blocks of flats of up to 20 storeys high erected. These towers reared up like giant signposts of a new age.

Amenities in the houses of the 1960s include electric, gas, or oil-fired central heating systems. Night storage heaters use current at off-peak times, and diffuse the stored heat during the day. Electrical heating is done with oil-fired radiators as well; under-floor heating and warm air blown through floor-level grills come from the same source. In the towns, grate fires are restricted to smokeless fuel, and in the near future open fires may not be used at all by forward-looking people.

Glancing back over the last 50 or 60 years, one can see a change of character in the general style of homes. For about a third of that period, the traditional frontage with curved bow or square bay windows, paired or single, was the accepted style for the everyday house. Some decoration around the doorway was frequently seen, with pilasters, even pillars, and a moulded pediment. A great deal of brickwork, both glazed and red, appeared in town houses and pierced weatherboards were still favoured in the larger buildings. In all cases, gutters and downpipes were of cast-iron, bearing an occasional lead rain-water head.

With the increasing use of concrete walls, built up with moulded blocks, plastering was necessary, and houses finished in light-coloured plaster predominated by 1935. It became the practice to standardise, not only in council houses; repetition was a growing trend. After 1945, this mass-production appearance became even more noticeable—in fact, some critics referred to 'rows of concrete boxes'. Before 1960, the bow front was out of favour with designers.

26

5   Stevenage 'New Town'

In most houses, flat casements with the picture-window were
seen, but there was a partial return to sash windows, unweighted,
with aluminium frames. Double-glazing was quite common, with
a vacuum between the layers of glass, so that outside conditions
did not fog the glass.

Private firms were doing highly profitable business in 1964 in
building large estates; former carpenters and painters reached
tycoon status as builders within a few years. This prosperity was
reflected in the workers, for at that time construction gangs of
tradesmen, with labourers, were building a house per week and
earning £50 each. In order to build quickly, hip or sloped roofs
were abandoned for the straight barn-type roof, where the timber-
ing was uncomplicated. High-speed work of that kind was badly
hit when the 'credit squeeze' of 1966-7 cut down all mortgage and
business-credit facilities for a time.

One distinguishing feature of the modern housing estate is the
absence of formal separation between gardens(5). It is not permitted to build high walls, and in most instances the only division
is a low post-and-wire fence. This might eventually lead to the
American system, where gardens are laid in front of the houses in

27

6   Modern living room

a continuous strip divided only by paths. It is a sign of the times that, on some estates, drives and garages take up as much space as the houses themselves.

There are some well-designed prefab and unit-construction plans on the market. Kitchen and bathroom, each completely fitted up, are lowered into position, and other units fixed to them. In other schemes, sections are bolted into place as sheets, as in the chalet-type dwelling entirely composed of plastic sheeting. 'Bricks' made of plastic offer a lighter, more durable house structure.

These ideas are not in general use; the great majority of house-buyers seem to prefer the solid brick house, especially as an ordinary house can be completed in three months. Quick-drying plaster has much reduced the waiting period before occupation can take place.

In business and professional buildings, the straight-line principle is maintained, with a basis of steel girders. For that reason our great cities are studded with towering glass-and-concrete office blocks, and our new schools display long stretches of tall windows. In both cases, the expanse of glass is a mixed blessing; light interiors mean roasting heat when the sun is on the glass.

Present-day design stresses the angular form. There is no wish to spend time in decorating the structure, and the result is functional severity. Of the 10 new buildings which won the 1966 awards of the Royal Institute of British Architects, only one design showed any relief from the angular—the Roman Catholic Church of the Good Shepherd, Nottingham. This design, by Gerald Goalen, contained some bizarre features, but it was not completely rigid in line.

Almost every new church displays the same tendency; gone are the Gothic features and the traditional outline, to be replaced by symbolic significance. Pre-cast concrete takes the place of carved stonework, thereby reducing building time considerably.

A report on the Liverpool Catholic Cathedral of Christ the King, designed by Sir Frederick Gibberd, shows that the concrete, stone, and glass building was completed on an existing foundation in five years. Its counterpart, the city's Anglican cathedral, was designed by Giles Gilbert Scott in traditional style, and is still unfinished, having been under construction since 1904. There is a great contrast between the new and the traditional outline; Scott's mediaeval tower is within sight of the truncated cone and lantern of the Catholic Cathedral.

It is safe to say that no previous half-century has shown such a revolution in outlook, design, and building methods. In some ways, human sensibilities tend to suffer through this mass medium. For instance, a child living on the twentieth storey of a block of flats cannot easily reach the street to make his way to a play centre, so a kind of isolation may result. This is an example of what can happen when large-scale planning takes no account of human reactions.

Chapter II
THE KITCHEN TRANSFORMED

I N spite of the great changes that have taken place in house design and building, they are not as remarkable as progress in the kitchen since the First World War. Yet there was a pleasant atmosphere in the farmhouse kitchen of those days. With its stone-flagged floor, gaunt black ceiling beams and heavy, ill-fitting door, it was a homely place (7).

Many farmers' wives still had the huge open hearth, with black iron firedogs supporting a big wood fire, and the wall ovens flanking the fireplace. It was fascinating to see baking done—the deep hollow in the wall, floor glowing with embers and roof whitened with heat. A long-handled paddle, called a 'peel', was used to put in and remove the baking vessels, and country people swore that there was no flavour like that of wall-oven baking. This was particularly true of bread; even today, feeble imitations styled 'farmhouse bread' are on sale.

That great fireplace was a centre of activity, decoration, and recreation. At intervals during the day, a perspiring wife organised the oven, a battery of crook-hung pots, and skillets on the fringe of the fire. Across the mouth of the huge chimney was fixed a stout iron bar, from which hung iron crooks with teeth throughout their length. These teeth allowed sliding crooks to engage at different heights according to the size of the hanging pot. Special open-fire vessels were used—a kettle with a long lever ('handymaid') attached to its handle for heat-free tipping, a slung frying-pan, and various boilers. All these were of cast-iron, and well blackened on the outside.

High above the fireplace, along the mantelpiece with its gathered strip of curtain material serving as a pelmet, were ranged the ornamental and utilitarian articles that had accumulated there. An old brass pestle and mortar stood by a tobacco jar and pipe rack; here were china figures, a pair of pewter candlesticks, and so on. On the wall over the mantel a pegged gun-rack supported favourite shotguns, and hanging on each side of the fireplace were gleaming horse-brasses and warming-pans. These might be half-hidden by

7 Farm kitchen, 1914

the high-backed, angular 'settles' which sheltered fireside sitters
from the fierce draughts drawn in by the wide chimney. It was an
old country idea to sweep the chimney by firing a gun up it. The
vibration of the shot certainly dislodged the soot, but the gunman
had to step back smartly to avoid being smothered.

Standing somewhere near the deep windows was a great
scrubbed pine table flanked by long oak forms. The other large
item of furniture was a tall, dark, old dresser bearing a load of
crockery. At mealtimes the long kitchen was full of life, with people
grouped all round the great table and hearty voices ringing. When
darkness fell, and hobnailed boots had been exchanged for
slippers, there was laughter and comfort around the blazing logs.
Perhaps a feeble lamb or piglet might share the warmth, bottle-fed
and wrapped in rags in the chimney corner.

In those farm kitchens where progress had arrived, the hearth
would be commanded by a big, cast-iron range, combining in one
unit all the facilities of the older style. On its ample top stood the
saucepans and boilers, its ovens cooked under control, and a
side boiler provided hot water. In the summer, the farmer's wife

31

sometimes used an oil cooker, which saved her having to work over the great range. It meant that she could no longer sit by the fire in the evenings, but no doubt the reduced work made up for that.

Throughout the village, in the workers' houses, the kitchen was often the only sitting room, a place in which to cook, eat, work, and, at times, bathe. Here a small, cast-iron cottage range was the focal point, around which the family sat, feet on the fender. In some cottages of the early 1920s the open hearth and the wall oven were still in use. A few of the better houses in the village had carbide gas lighting, from the source that supplied the street lamps, but the majority of the villagers used paraffin lamps, which gave a pleasant, mellow light.

There was a legacy of Victorian feeling in the town kitchen of that time. Though it had the advantage of more convenience, it was the Cinderella of the rooms. If it was not below ground, it was situated somewhere at the back of the house, with little or no view of the outside world. It was not thought necessary to study the position of the kitchen. Even in moderately well-to-do houses it was often operated by servants and, if there were no servants, a position at the back was still considered good enough for the cooking-place. Thus servant or housewife was condemned to work in a room sometimes totally cut off from the sunlight, where a brick wall might be the only prospect.

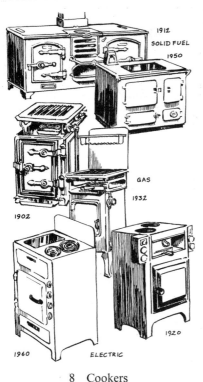

8 Cookers

In the town there was a wider choice of cooking appliances (8). True, the cast-iron range still held its place, but coal-gas cookery was quite common. It had been pioneered nearly 100 years before in 1824, when the Aetna Iron Works, in the Liverpool district, produced a griller for use with gas. After much

32

experiment, James Sharp of Southampton produced a curious cylindrical gas cooker in 1851, which was shown at a trade exhibition after it had been rejected by the Crystal Palace authorities.

Sharp's cooker was a success in America, but not in England. However, increased burner efficiency, based on Bunsen's work, made gas cooking quite popular by 1880, and the 1918 cooker had recognisable modern features—flat top rings, a plate rack, and a plate-warming drawer. A pan of water placed under the cooker was intended to absorb any smell of gas, though even now this is difficult to eliminate completely.

About 1930 an oven-control dial was introduced for gas cookers. This was named 'Regulo', and cookery books from that time added the appropriate Regulo readings for their recipes. It was an excellent idea providing the gas pressure remained consistent. If the pressure varied, cooking became more difficult.

In spite of the advantages of gas cooking, the old cast-iron range continued to be used for a surprisingly long time; it was still being fitted into new houses in the post-1945 years. This overlap was repeated when the gas cooker was supplemented by electric models. At first the approach was cautious. Experiments between 1880 and 1890 had shown that the idea was practicable, but few women would harbour an electric cooker in their kitchen, and it was rarely seen until 1914. Even at that time, there was little attraction in its appearance, for electric kitchen equipment was usually black. By 1920 the cooker was a practical proposition, looking like a disguised gas stove, but it was not really popular. Much of the distrust was due to the invisible heat—fire or gas jets could be seen, but the mysterious black monster showed no outward signs of activity.

Cooking was the most important kitchen work, but laundry and dish-washing came close behind. Mechanical clothes-washers had been the target of inventors since the late eighteenth century, but few people had used the machines concerned. In most of them the main feature was a pair of washboards in corrugated wood, the boards being moved across each other by means of a lever, but scarcely five per cent of England's washing was done in this way until about 1920. 'Tub and scrub' was the watchword, with soaked, reddened hands and aching backs for those dealing with most domestic washing. When the tub work had been done and the wash was on the line, the vagaries of English weather represented another hazard.

After the wash, the ironing; for centuries British housewives had used the 'flat-iron', a solid iron to be heated on fire or stove. Several heating ideas were used during the nineteenth century. A 'box-iron' was a hollow casing into which a heated iron shape was placed, while other shapes were heating in readiness.

There was a charcoal iron, which had a little brazier to keep it hot, and in 1880 the gas-heated iron was used, with a flexible tube attached. Electric irons were developed between 1900 and 1909, but like most electrical devices they were regarded very warily.

Other efforts to mechanise the kitchen included plate-washing devices, none of which were really successful. Their action was usually based on a tub with rotating metal blades arranged at the bottom, so that the hot water was forced up between the rows of plates which were placed on their edges. One of the difficulties was to keep the water supply hot enough to scald the plates, and another to make the water pass through with force. Few people thought the expense and uncertainty worth while when human dish-washers were cheap and plentiful.

A handy item in kitchen progress was the developed refrigerator (*10*). Among the technical advances of the nineteenth century, ice-making had been done with liquids having a high boiling point. Ammonia was used by Ferdinand Carré in 1859 and Rees Reece in 1869. Carré's machine had a boiler and a refrigerator connected by a tube. In the boiler, a 75 per cent solution of ammonia was heated to 130–150°C, so that the ammonia vapour created high pressure. When the vapour expanded through the tube into the refrigerator, the cold water circulating around the latter reduced the ammonia to liquid again, and the boiler was immersed in cold water. As the boiler temperature fell, lowering the pressure in the machine, the ammonia vaporised quickly, and by absorbing the heat from its surroundings produced intense cold.

In two hours Carré's machine made two pounds of ice—a slow process, so the ordinary ice-box remained in use until the early twentieth century. At that time a practical kitchen refrigerator was being sought. Here American makers led the way from about 1917, and over 20,000 American housewives had refrigerators by 1923. In these, brine was circulated by means of a small electric motor, but few were to be seen in England.

THE KITCHEN TRANSFORMED

Kitchen reform took place only in progressive houses. At each stage there was a long trail of survivals, old-style households, and outdated equipment. However, those who adopted new ideas did have a little influence. For instance, the ancient dresser, loaded with china and knick-knacks, was being superseded by the kitchen cabinet soon after 1920. At first this was a conversion—doors fitted to the upper shelves, a flap-down hinged table, and the drawers hygienically lined to hold bread and cookery supplies. This became a free-standing portable unit with glass door.

A bold step in design made at the same time was the arrangement of a small annexe off the kitchen as the breakfast recess. Previously it had been thought extremely low-class to eat in the kitchen, but after the First World War it was obvious that a new social pattern was emerging. There were far fewer domestic servants, for girls had found during the war that they could do other, less menial, work. This meant that the middle-class housewife who formerly employed a 'cook-general' might have to do her own work. Many were also forced to do so through shortage of money.

A servantless kitchen had been shrewdly foreseen 50 years before by Catherine Beecher, sister of Harriet Beecher Stowe (the author of *Uncle Tom's Cabin*). Miss Beecher actually designed the first streamlined kitchen in 1869, to meet the needs of a possible servantless age. In the Beecher kitchen design, a familiar pattern of sink, drainer, work-top, and under-cupboards was arranged for convenience, and a range of shelves on the wall above provided more storage. These were difficult to reach, and another ill-planned item was the separate stove room. Still, the designer was a pioneer of studied placing, where all before had been haphazard.

During the period 1920–35, the slow surges of change were being felt in the kitchen world. First on the list of needs was the matter of position. Any observant designer could see that in a great number of old and new houses the kitchen had been granted little attention. Like the toilet of former days, it seemed to be squeezed into any out-of-the-way place that remained vacant after the living rooms and bedrooms had been sited. As long as it could be served by a back door its outlook and atmosphere counted for little. This was an obvious survival from the long years when the kitchen was the place of servants, to which the mistress descended only on set occasions.

With the decline in servants and the increasing tendency for the wife to run the kitchen herself, concern for conditions grew. At length the architect came to realise that the kitchen was not merely an attachment but the operative centre of the house. That in itself was a great step forward.

Next came the reform of kitchen design and the dawn of domestic time-and-motion study in the late 1920s. A number of important points were worked out for a practical kitchen. It must not be so big that long walks between sink, cooker, and working surfaces were involved, nor so small that it became steamy. (This problem brought into the kitchen an electric exhausting fan, set in a window pane, to draw out smells and steam.) Preferably there should be windows in two walls, facing east and south respectively, in order to let the sun in right through the day. Artificial lighting was poor in most kitchens, with a centre light that lit only the centre. At the sink, the housewife stood in her own light, and when using the oven her shadow was cast into it.

Before 1930, a number of architects were using the 'continuous working surface'. This saved unnecessary walking by providing flat tops on the cooker, refrigerator, and storage units. Though these were experiments, the true kitchen reformation did not occur until after the Second World War. In all directions, up-to-date form, materials, and planning revitalised the heart of the house. Gloomy corners were banished by the use of light colours on the walls, in paint, tiles, or sheets of laminated plastic. Sink duty was lightened by a wide picture-window over the taps, flowers upon the tiled window-ledge, and gay curtains.

Though hundreds of new houses were still being fitted with 'porcelain enamel' pottery sinks and wooden draining-boards, the elegant 'sink unit' was on exhibition in 1947. It had a range of low-level shelved cupboards, with a one-piece metal top; sink bowl and single or double drainers were pressed out of a sheet of steel. There was a choice of finish, in 'vitreous' (fused-glass) enamel, with a range of colours, or 'stainless steel'. Eventually the old-type sink with wooden draining-boards was declared illegal.

Opinions differed very widely about the two types of sink unit, as each had a drawback. If the vitreous enamel was chipped, there was no easy way of concealing the damage. Stainless-steel tops did not suffer from this disadvantage, but it was hard to maintain the original bright finish. Unless the metal was polished frequently, it came to look rather like those sheets of zinc that some people used to protect wooden drainers.

A useful fitting that was first applied to the sink unit about 1950 was the mixer tap. For many years the hot and cold taps had stood side by side, mingling their deliveries in the sink. Mixer taps did the mingling before delivery, the two taps being connected with a common delivery spout. One disadvantage was that, if one wished to draw drinking water after turning off the hot tap, tank water was left in the mixer pipe. In the new mixer tap of 1963, the actual delivery spout had two outlets, hot and cold, so that the mixture took place at the outlet.

After 1945, there was a wide choice of domestic water-heaters. Most old-style kitchen ranges connected with the boiler had been replaced with up-to-date cooker-heaters, such as Aga or Rayburn, before 1950. They could be kept going day and night, with low fuel consumption, and their vitreous-enamel, wipe-clean surfaces were a relief to the housewife after the old blackleaded range.

Apart from fuel-burners, very efficient gas and electric heaters were also available. They could be fixed as local water-heaters over kitchen sink or bath in houses with no circulating hot-water system. A common arrangement of about 1948 was a back-boiler behind the lounge fireplace, for use in winter, and an electric immersion heater in the hot-water tank for use when there was no fire.

There were two forms of immersion heater, acting like red-hot pokers in the hot-water tank. A long heater had three or four elements, extending almost the length of the tank, which warmed the whole of its contents. If only a small quantity was needed in a short time, there was a short heater of about a quarter the length. This was set into the top of the tank almost from side to side, and heated only the near-by water.

This was the period of the streamlined kitchen of clinical appearance, from composition-tiled floor to insulated ceiling. Around three sides of an up-to-date kitchen in 1952 was ranged an almost unbroken stretch of wipeable, flat-top surfaces. At the sink unit came the only interruption in the smooth run, and the cupboards below were all recessed to allow close-up standing while working.

A typical range of units would have refrigerator, deep-freeze for long-term food storage, cupboards, sink unit, and gas or electric cooker. Above, on the walls of each side, hanging cupboards in line provided extra storage. In order to prevent upper surfaces from catching dust, on the rows of high cupboards 'space fillers' were fitted to block up the unused space above the cupboards. Similar fillers were put into the angles of the lower cupboards. All these fittings were in pastel shades, with stainless steel strips to mask the joints between the cupboard sections.

In the old-style kitchen a great drawback was the isolation of the housewife, who was cut off from the rest of the house. Several postwar designs showed new methods of overcoming the barrier, such as the serving hatch giving quick access to the dining area. Another idea, which meant great changes in house design, was the 'open plan' (9), where living quarters and kitchen were not separated by walls. In a central pillar were placed the cooker on the kitchen side and the lounge fireplace on the other. Some designs featured a folding screen partition between kitchen and dining room, and one in particular, of 1949, had the kitchen ceiling raised to upper-floor level to take off cooking smells.

In general kitchen equipment of the 1950s the keynote was

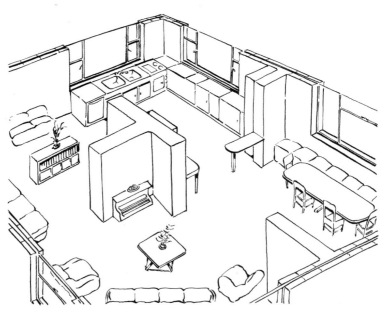

9   Open plan kitchen

vitreous enamel. This provided the glossy wiping surfaces of cooker, sink, and refrigerator, as well as the increasingly popular washing machine(*10*). Though the latter was a comparative new-comer, a reasonably priced electric washing machine had been on the English market since a few years before the war. Mass production had brought the machine within reach of hire-purchasers. This earlier model had a little wringer fitted over the top, but the postwar development of the spin-dryer made the wringer unnecessary. By 1950 the combination would tumble the clothes automatically in soap-suds, rinse them repeatedly, and spin out most of the water. Spin-dried clothes still need to be hung out for final drying, but ironing has been reduced by drip-dry, non-iron materials.

10   Washing machines and refrigerators

Perhaps the most significant change in the kitchen is its social status. This is a streamlined age, a period of time-and-motion study, of impatience with ceremony. For that reason the practice of serving the family meal in the dining room is declining. Of course, there were millions of people in the past who ate in their kitchens, but they were looked down on for it. There was probably a good, practical reason for this apparent snobbery—the kitchen diner often had to contend with the old pottery sink under his elbow, a black-finished cooking range behind him, and a dresser at his flank.

In these enlightened days the kitchen is one of the most attractive rooms, especially at breakfast time, with an east-facing window. Central light fittings have given way to strip lighting, or arranged light points.

39

We have already shown that the dining recess was introduced about 1923, and this plan was developed in the 1960s when some architects combined the kitchen and dining room. In the early part of the decade there was also a trend away from the super-chromium, clinical kitchen to a more homely décor—wood-panelling, decorative features, and items of Victoriana. Here the idea was not to link dining room and kitchen, but to make the kitchen look like a dining room(*11*).

There were immense resources at the housewife's command. Her electric cooker could be clock-regulated, and not affected by variations of supply that occurred at peak load periods. These cookers were fitted with compensators to adjust the controls at need. Kitchenware was a far cry from the black cast-iron and enamel of the early twentieth century. It progressed through aluminium, itself a light and convenient material, to the age of plastics. Polythene and similar materials provided tough, gaily coloured utensils which were hygienic and easily cleaned. This material was used not only for pans, but for actual implements like the wall tin-opener and the food-mixer. There is scarcely

11   Modern kitchen

any limit to the uses of plastics in the kitchen.

It is interesting to note that the product of a society in a hurry, the pressure cooker, was still not out of favour by the late 1960s, though it had suffered a decline earlier in that period. Pressure cooking offered rapid-action cooking for the worker-housewife—potatoes cooked in six minutes instead of 20, stew in 20 minutes rather than two hours.

12   Dish-washer

Further time-saving was achieved by 'instant' products—coffee, pie-mixes, dehydrated foods, and the enormous range of frozen foods that made for less time at the cooker. In 1966 a well-known canned-food firm issued a big advertisement detailing its products, and headed, 'Why bother to cook?'

Even washing-up was mechanised by the further development of dish-washing machines during the 1950s(12). These were the subject of much criticism. About 1965 a famous research group published their findings on various dish-washers; according to the group most machines were not fully efficient. Their superheated water-jets did not always clean forks, and traces of food some-times remained on plates.

At no time in its history had the kitchen been accorded so much scientific thought. In June 1969, the chairman of the Electrical Development Association spoke strongly on the need for bigger kitchens to house the equipment that was to come. All the existing devices for cooking, freezing, and washing were likely to be expanded in size and number, said the chairman. Progress had been made in work on an electronic oven, for extra-rapid heat-ing of refrigerated meals, and on a thermostatic probe to deal with roasting temperatures. With a control panel in the kitchen, the housewife could adjust temperatures for the house itself, and switch on frost protection in attic, garage, and greenhouse. Closed-circuit television would watch the front door and the nursery.

One humble need that was mentioned by the chairman con-cerned waste disposal. Sink pulverising units, which ground up the waste for washing down the outlet, did not meet the case, and the chairman's suggestion of an incinerator would have meant an air-pollution problem in towns.

In 1961 a newspaper columnist praised the advances of her time—the rotating wall-hung dish-washer, a new eye-level oven, with a button-controlled rack for grilling or baking. At the same time a 'revolutionary invention' by a housewife was reported—cooking by means of passing a current through food immersed in cold water. In four seconds a sausage was cooked, while the water remained cold. However, nothing more about this idea has been reported.

Just over a year later an exhibition kitchen showed a division into three sections—preparation and cooking, eating and storage, washing-up and clearing. In the first section was a double sink, while the stainless-steel top had inset electric rings, and a teak chopping board was supplied. Eating was actually done in the dining room next to the kitchen, but an electric hotplate was installed there to keep the food simmering after it had been passed through the button-controlled serving hatch. Under the washing-up area were filing-cabinet-style drawers for dishes, and the top cupboards held glasses and light china.

It was calculated in 1964 that 36 per cent of British homes had refrigerators, and that 100,000 shops sold frozen foods. This was discussed at a conference of frozen food producers, and a directive was issued on the length of time frozen foods could be stored at home in the freezing compartment of a home refrigerator. As a result, frozen foods and refrigerators were graded with stars according to the length of time they could be kept fresh. One star denoted a week, two stars a month, and three stars three months. This is an example of another feature of the kitchen age—advice on every aspect of kitchen-work as well as the services of scientific brains are at the disposal of the housewife.

Chapter III
FAMILY LIFE AND THE ADVANCE
OF WOMEN

Most people who are interested in history are able to visualise the 'traditional' English family. This word conjures up the family album, Victorian 'home' journals, and the quiet Sunday. It is true that the Victorian outlook of the middle-class home persisted until the early years of George V, so that family life in 1914 was much the same as that of 20 years before. It was an age of gracious living for those with a reasonable income—a pattern of domestic quietness, sombre interior, heavy, dark furniture, and curtain furbelows.

In the drawing room, firelight winked on the gleaming brasswork, and the father of the family sat comfortably in his draped armchair. Opposite his throne, mother peered in the shrouded light at a delicate piece of lace, and instructed small daughter on the stitches involved. Restrained activity of various kinds occupied the rest of the family—decorous, and with a genteel air bred of constant training.

Family meals were substantial, if dull for the younger members, who were directed to eat up before leaving the table. It was still the era of brimstone and treacle as a spring posset, eaten with distaste. At the same time, the home atmosphere, though repressive, was reassuringly solid. Youthful troubles and fears could be confided to mother, who would discuss them with father, and dispense comfort. When young critics sit in judgement on the home life of that time, they forget that the outlook was suited to the period. A boy of 1914 would be as out of place in a present-day home as our adolescents would be in his.

Among the 'working class', a term usually applied to manual workers, family life had a different meaning. Their welfare, even their lives, depended upon the well-being and perseverance of grown-up male members of the family. If it was only the father who supported the home, its position might be even more precarious. In their poor cottage, with the minimum of food and comfort, a difference of a shilling in the weekly wage could be

13   Poor East End family

serious. An ill-tempered, brutal, or drunken father meant terror and insecurity among the family, particularly as there was little official restraint upon his treatment of wife or children.

On the other hand, if the father strove to provide for his family, poverty bound them even more closely together. Scanty fare and poor surroundings were borne cheerfully, if they were shared with love. When they could all make some outing together, perhaps a day of gathering blackberries, the simple pleasure brought more happiness than the most elaborate entertainment could have done. In the peaceful countryside, as yet little disturbed by mechanical traffic, that most placid of occupations was something to remember. With the sun bringing out the heady scent of the gleaming black fruit, the springy grass underfoot, and their own kin around them, those children of the poor knew happiness.

Upon that slow-moving world of 1914 came a great leveller that shocked family life from its even course. From thousands of households, rich and poor, menfolk were gone, and the family, like a crippled animal, had to struggle along as best it could. It was

44

an unnatural era; father, brother, or son missing from the fireside, leaving anxiety and prayer behind, and only letters from far away to act as a link. At long intervals the lost one came home for a too-short stay. Everyone was frantic to make the utmost of the flying hours; then there was a parting more bitter than the first. Among the poorer families the scanty Service allowance had to be augmented in some fashion, the meagre rations eked out with something that would fill hungry stomachs; so the family crept its fumbling way.

When the four bleak years were over, and no heartbreaking telegram had been received, the homecoming might still be that of a crippled man, smitten by wounds or exposure. Family joy was mixed with pity and sorrow, and further adjustment of the way of life; the head of the family forced to lie helpless while his family worked for him.

That tremendous upheaval did more than rob the country of a million menfolk; it began a change in family relationships that was never to be reversed. During the four years, the women of the nation had served as never before. Women of all classes, rich and

14 Women munition workers—based on photograph of 1914

15   Mrs Pankhurst in 1913

poor, old and young, had plunged in to take the places of the men in the fighting line. In the mines, on the railways, with coal wagons and postman's bicycles, at factory bench (*14*), and on the farm, Englishwomen did noble service.

A great example was given by an association that had been a bitter thorn in the Government's side—the militant suffragettes, those hardy female campaigners from all walks of life who had urged the vote for women. More than 10 years before the war, Mrs Emmeline Pankhurst (1858–1928) had founded the Women's Social and Political Union, in 1903, with the object of gaining the vote. Mrs Pankhurst (*15*) was ably supported by her daughters Christabel (then aged 23) and Sylvia (21).

Suffragettes were of two classes—the constitutionals, who hoped to succeed by representation, and the militants, whose forceful campaign was launched by Mrs Pankhurst in 1906. Their activities were manifold. Some members showered M.P.s in the House with leaflets demanding votes, and one minister was bombarded with bags of soot and flour. There were screaming women who chained themselves to Hyde Park railings and threw away the padlock keys; women who set fire to St Catherine's Church in Hatcham; and those who smashed shop windows, crying 'Votes for women!'

This movement caused trouble in many peaceful families, where rebellious women threw in their hands with the suffragettes. One nasty feature of those turbulent times was the ill-treatment of the campaigners during their demonstrations. These women were often very roughly handled by the police, and ruffians in the crowd would take the opportunity of punching and kicking them.

A large number of suffragettes were imprisoned on charges of causing a disturbance, but the hardier members went on hunger strike. In dealing with this, the prison authorities arranged for forcible feeding. Stalwart women warders brought a stretcher trolley and straps to the cell of the hunger striker. She was secured, her mouth was prised open, and nourishing soup was passed in through a tube.

If a suffragette became ill in prison through fasting, she could be released temporarily under the Prisoners, Temporary Discharge for Health Act of 1913 (the 'Cat and Mouse' Act). She returned to complete the sentence when she was better. It was not uncommon for this to-and-fro movement to be repeated several times. Mrs Pankhurst herself was rearrested 12 times, but she served only 30 days of a three-year sentence. All this activity made the militant women a household word throughout England. Best-known of all was Miss Emily Davidson, who threw herself under the King's horse, Anmer, at Tattenham Corner during the 1913 Derby. Miss Davidson died of her injuries four days later.

When the war broke out nothing had been gained; the authorities remained firm, but Mrs Pankhurst patriotically directed the furious energies of her followers into working for the Government, instead of against it. This brought the spearhead of the great female labour force into action. The noble work of women in industry gained the vote for those over 30, by the Qualification

16   Lady Astor in Plymouth election, 1923

of Women Act, 1918. Ten years later women of 21 were included. This was described as the 'flapper' vote, 'flapper' being the name applied to lively post-1918 girls.

Thus, thousands of mothers, daughters, and wives were led into the tasks of men, often sacrificing health and good looks in the munitions works. Many of them had never worked before and the experience of being self-supporting and independent gave them a feeling of freedom. Some of them even joined the Women's Services, such as the Women's Auxiliary Army Corps—an unprecedented move. Though, of course, there were many thousands of women who continued simply to make homes for their families, and who were unaffected by the new freedom, the feminist spirit was aroused. Never again would women as a class allow themselves to be regarded as inferiors by the all-powerful male.

As if to hammer home that lesson, the first woman M.P. made her way into the House in 1919—Lady Astor (*16*), who succeeded

17 Early policewomen

her husband as Member for Plymouth when he inherited his father's peerage. It is curious that both the Member and her husband were American-born, Lord Astor's father having become a naturalised Briton in 1900. Next on the ladder of fame was Miss Margaret Bondfield, a Labour politician and a trade unionist. She served in the House for the first time in 1923, and she was the first woman to enter the Cabinet; Miss Bondfield was Minister of Labour from 1929 to 1931.

These were prominent women, but many of their less distinguished sisters helped to bring on the labour troubles of the 1920s. Women were in the forefront to stay, and during that postwar period this

18   Modern policewoman and potential suicide

was made clear. Formerly, middle-class women had been confined to the home, their education wasted by exclusion from the men's world; now they thrust themselves into it. It was the Sex Disqualification Removal Act of 1919 that made this possible. Through that concession women could take civil and judicial positions, or enter on careers—accountancy, banking, the law. Even the Civil Service was open to them at all but the highest levels, though not on equal pay.

Some women had been in Government employment since 1888, for in that year the first two 'lady typewriters' were in the Inland Revenue Department at Whitehall. Not more than 20 typists were to be found in the whole country. In Whitehall, the two pioneers were segregated, their work being passed to them through a hatch. When they went to draw their pay, they were escorted by two male messengers. By 1915, there were 600 women typists, and women eventually proved faster then men. In the international typing contests of the 1930s, the winner was always a woman.

Men-about-town of 1914 must have rubbed their eyes when members of the new Women's Police Force appeared on duty.

They were hideously ill-clad—long, heavy skirts, long, leather-belted tunic, boots, and a stiff helmet (a squashed version of the male type)(*17*). Mary Sophia Allen was Britain's first uniformed policewoman, one of the founders of women police in London. As a suffragette, she had once been gaoled for trying to force her way into the House. On 17 December 1964 Commandant Allen died at the age of 86, in a Croydon nursing home.

Policewomen had become familiar to the public by the end of the First World War. A photograph of 1921 taken on the bank of the Serpentine shows a female constable, in her unlovely drapery, chasing and caning a group of small boys for bathing in the nude.

Such changes brought a new atmosphere into family life. Womenfolk ceased to be mere domestic ornaments and began to make a contribution to national affairs. In May 1930 a 25-year-old secretary from Hull, Amy Johnson(*19*), astonished the world by flying solo from Croydon to Australia in 19½ days—the first lone woman pilot. She was a keen though not particularly skilful flyer, with great mechanical ability. Her extraordinary courage was even more remarkable in view of the numerous mishaps to her plane. In one incident she broke the airscrew, but she carried a spare strapped outside the fuselage!

Amy Johnson leaped into fame, even to the extent of having the song-writers hail her 'Amy, wonderful Amy'. She followed up her adventure with a record-breaking flight to the Cape. These events were recalled in 1967 when Miss Johnson's biography was written by Constance Babington Smith, top woman interpreter in Photographic Intelligence. At the same time, work was proceeding on a musical based on the same theme, and the way in which public

19   Amy Johnson in 1930

imagination had been caught by that symbol of the emancipation of women.

More revelations were to come, for nine years after that historic Australia flight a new generation of mothers, sweethearts, and wives were to step into the breach left by a new generation of men at war.

This mass advance by women was to complete the break-up in the former pattern of the family. Work in farm and factory, hospital and welfare centre, and service with the forces opened fresh fields of independence. With their tenacity and skilful management, those housewives who contributed by bringing up families and feeding workers proved themselves the home front heroines of the war. Uncounted miles were covered from shop to shop, tracking down the rumour of some foodstuffs 'off the ration'. Inventive genius worthy of a professor was expended in preparing nourishing meals. Small wonder that, when the six years of strain were over, Englishwomen were a different race.

One of the most noticeable results of wartime was the continuance of whole or part-time work by women with no real need to do it. This was due to the independent spirit. Women who had been receiving an income of their own did not care to return to the narrow world of kitchen and nursery. For that reason, their husbands had to adjust their own outlook. It was no longer a question of breadwinner and wife, but of joint income. Much thought was given to this. Once again women had proved their immense value in the ranks of workers, and in peacetime employers wished to keep their services. Equal pay for equal work was much canvassed. In 1947 the United Kingdon representatives approved Article 23 as laid down by the United Nations Assembly: 'Everyone without any discrimination has a right to equal pay for equal work.'

In the professions a long struggle took place over the drive for equality. Until a few years before the date of that resolution schoolmistresses who married had to give up teaching, but in the late 1950s the authorities very grudgingly agreed to a long-term adjustment of women teachers' salaries, so that in the end equal pay would become a reality in this profession.

Apart from the matter of an independent income, there was another good reason why women of the postwar years went to work. It was a period of house-hunting. Though houses were being built for sale, many young engaged couples were looking for homes to rent. Unfurnished houses or flats were most difficult to find, so the solution was to marry without a home and live with parents. This was a reason for the young wife to continue going out to work, instead of being an accessory in someone else's home.

By the 1960s the working wife had become a feature so common as to pass unnoticed. In countless homes the mother, once the permanent centre of the household, was out at work all day, so that the children could not get in if they went home in an emergency. This meant a completely changed course of household affairs. Where husband and wife were both at work, tasks in the house had to be done together in the evening, at the weekend, or on the mid-week half-day. When it first became available, the pressure cooker was very valuable in this hurried atmosphere, though its popularity later declined. Still, the organisation of meals was a demanding task for the working mother.

This change of the woman's place in everyday life greatly speeded the decline of the traditional family circle. No mother could easily play the part of a placid central figure, providing understanding and comfort, when she was harassed with the thought of an evening's housework after a day of outside employment. Shopping under normal circumstances was a necessary labour, but shopping on the run during the lunch-hour or before nine in the morning was one of the crosses of the worker-wife-mother.

Where formerly many wives had gone into employment because they were bored or were living with parents-in-law, they had different reasons for doing so in the 1960s. A double income helped to pay for a new house—this was the age of house-buying, not house-hunting – and to buy things that they wanted. Kitchen appliances like washing machines and refrigerators verged on the essential, and the car was a leading requirement. The money earned by a working wife helped to acquire such objects, and in any case the prospects of a housebound existence appalled many active, well-educated wives, who were frank enough to admit that they hated housework. 'I should go mad if I had to stay at home' was a remark quite commonly heard.

One reason for the shortage of young domestic servants was the advance of feminine education, with the wider range of opportunity which that brought. Girls of low-income families were no longer forced to go into domestic work as the only outlet. Openings in other fields of employment drew them away from the kitchen sink!

In making a survey of English society since 1914, it is plain that the contrast between the 1914 family and the family of 50 years later is largely due to the progress of women. This, with the equality drive, has changed very greatly women's place in society. Instead of being sheltered by her husband, the present-day

20   Mrs Barbara Castle, Secretary for Employment and Productivity, 1968

woman frequently takes the place of protector and organiser of the family. Women Ministers in important Cabinet posts (20), women judges, women doctors, all help to keep feminine abilities before the eyes of the nation. However, something has been lost by the masterful trend, and male courtesy has declined. In crowded public vehicles it is rare to see a man offering his seat to a woman, the philosophy being that, if women claim equal rights, they should expect to be treated as equals, too.

Women are being urgently sought by the Minister of Education to fill the ranks of teachers—those who left the classroom to raise families which are now at school are earnestly requested to consider returning. This applies to women trained in other professions as well, where top-rank positions have been allotted to them. In this connection, the critical male has cast doubts on female fitness for posts of great importance. It has been said that women are too easily swayed by emotional and temperamental influences, and that middle-aged female executives are completely unpredictable. Against this must be balanced the countless capable and even super-efficient professional women, whose services are invaluable.

Chapter IV
CHANGES IN FASHION

WOMEN of 1914 suffered from the pangs of transition. Those who rebelled against the image of the sweet and dainty frilled creature were striving to create a more realistic woman, but most of the others were still slaves to convention in dress. They were oppressed by the mass of 'woman's crowning glory', shot through with countless hairpins and topped by a hat loaded with flowers and grapes. In the hat itself were more pins— long steel affairs like stilettos with ornamental heads, nasty weapons in the hands of infuriated women.

Any survey of dress styles reveals that in the early twentieth century several fashion levels existed. At the top were the up-to-the-minute *élégantes*, followed by the more timid who provided a pale reflection. Next came the smart but outdated styles, retained by those with will-power enough to keep the clothes that they liked. Lower levels comprised the worker-fashionables, with 'inexpensive' renderings of more or less current modes, and, particularly in the country, the frankly behind-the-times 'best clothes', perhaps 20 years out of date and kept in mothballs.

For this reason, the 1914 period was one of variety. At that time, the tradesmen were gaining in their frantic battle against the hobble skirt—those wretched things which took only a quarter of the normal amount of cloth, with hems scarcely a yard around. Rival skirt forms, classical, flared, and peg-top, were paraded before the bewildered public. Those women who clung to the gracious former days still sported the wide-brimmed hat, sometimes extending beyond the shoulders, but there was a move towards a close, high-crowned model, with a broad ribbon, and a large pom-pom at the side. Lace was still widely employed; entire blouses of lace, with loose bodice and magyar-type sleeves were much favoured.

Though the First World War brought women into active national service, it would be a mistake to assume that all interest in fashionable clothes declined. Naturally the great patriotic surge drew the public's affectionate regard to the woman worker, but those women who were the lilies of the field served as living reminders that beauty and grace were still there, despite the rigours of wartime.

Among the workers, where utility was the keynote, a kind of uniform austerity prevailed. For those tending factory machines, with whirling belts and pulleys, it was soon obvious that long hair was a menace; a worker could be scalped if her hair became caught in a belt. This prospect led to a universal shortening of hair, to just below the ears. A similar revolution took place in skirt lengths; in general the hem was seven or eight inches from the ground. In the ugly and unbecoming Services uniform the same measure was adopted, for the same reason—greater freedom.

Fashionable circles kept to the feminine line, and the well-dressed woman favoured the draped, peg-topped skirt (full at the hips and tapering to a narrow hemline). A two-tiered tunic completed the *ensemble* for afternoon wear, while some women wore a small train. Tunic styles, evidently a military influence, were popular during the early war years, but by 1916 the skirt was widely flared, and the classical trend declined. A waisted, three-quarter-length coat worn over the skirt still gave a faint tunic effect, with wide collar and deep hem.

When the modish woman was walking, she usually wore what might be described as boots. They were really dainty, high-heeled shoes of patent leather, with high, laced tops in kid or a similar material, and light coloured (22). If shoes were worn outdoors, light cloth gaiters might be buttoned over them, as the shoes were strapped, with a low front. Silk stockings were a luxury, so most women wore cotton or lisle. A lady's accessories for outdoors

21 1914: Tailored suit, walking dress, and afternoon dress

55

22 Women's clothes, 1915–16

would include a slim parasol or umbrella, with elbow-gloves if she wore a short-sleeved dress, and she might carry the new underarm handbag.

By 1914, the up-to-date hair-style had drawn away from the Edwardian pompadour, though that was still to be seen after the war (*24*). A much more simple coiffure was in vogue, with a parting in a loose, waved style, and a bun at the nape. For some years previously, M. Marcel's style of waving (the 'Marcel wave') had been known in England—in fact, English hair-dressers gave Marcel an illuminated address in 1908. He had begun in business with ordinary crimping tongs in Paris about 1890, and, having developed a particular style of dexterous arrangement with waving, he became the most exclusive hairdresser in the city by 1895.

Actual permanent waving was originated by a German, Karl Nessler, who began with tongs but graduated to electrical apparatus. In his London premises at Oxford Street, the hairdresser advertised 'Nestlé Permanent Waving', and he enjoyed great success from 1904 to 1914. Though Nessler was interned as an enemy alien, he escaped to America, where his system brought him a fortune.

Most smart women used some cosmetics, and they were indebted to a face-powder recipe used by the 'Jersey Lily'. She was Lily Langtry, an American-born actress of New Jersey, who was famous both for her beauty and for her art. Miss Langtry's powder was made with great care. Melted lanolin was forced as a spray through fine mesh, while powdered talc (steatite) was blown in to mix with the spray. After mixing, the powder was passed hundreds of times between pairs of rollers, where fluting was opposed to bristles. Flesh tints for blondes were produced by adding carmine, and in brunette mixtures burnt umber or siena provided tints. Having been sifted through fine gauze, the powder was refined between plush-covered rollers, and scented by forcing it through a funnel with finely powdered violet root, or similar perfume.

Not all prewar cosmetics were as harmless as Miss Langtry's. A cheap product named 'violet powder' was made of scented starch, which tended to cause blackheads. There was another injurious product on sale, known as 'bloom', which set on the face like enamel and could not be moved with water. Face packs of mutton fat or prepared fuller's earth were employed, and the skin was treated with salicyclic acid dusting powder. During the early twentieth century rouge preparations had been refined a great deal, so the smart woman of 1914 used 'solid lip rouge', not in stick form, but made of carthamine from the safflower (an East Indian flower). Powdered talc and gum arabic formed the base of the rouge.

It is strange that eye make-up was extremely crude, when other preparations were so carefully composed. Eye cosmetics were little more than lamp-black and gum arabic. These were employed a good deal after 1911, through the influence of the Russian ballet in London. Other toilet accessories included red scented oil with beeswax as nail varnish (solid varnish was available), and various tooth powders. In most cases these were made of crushed charcoal, areca nuts, and cuttle-fish bone.

At the time of the First World War, men's clothes were going through a nondescript stage. They had outlived the time when the City was full of top-hats—only bank messengers provided a sprinkling of these by 1914—and were in the age of the mixture suit.

Among the photographs of civilians outside the War Office and the 'House' in early August 1914 can be seen a fair cross-section of men's clothes (23). As it was still summer weather, two-thirds of the men wore straw boaters; most of the remainder had flat caps, trilbies, or bowlers, with the occasional top-hat. Not a man was without a hat. All the jackets were long, with a vent at the back, and most suits were dark, with waistcoats. Here and there a sporty light suit could be seen, with a light cardigan instead of a waistcoat.

As this was a transition period, there was much variation in the

type of collar to be seen in a crowd of men. Some elderly citizens had the old tall collar, with the tie knotted low; there were low stiff collars, the single, wing collar, and also some kind of soft collar. One interesting thing about the crowds was that there were few moustaches to be seen, though we think of that as an age of moustaches. A great proportion of the men wore boots, some of patent leather with cloth tops, but there were a number of shoes, some with crêpe or rubber soles. Boys in the crowds showed a fair variety of clothing—Norfolk jackets of the type favoured by Edward VII, knickerbockers and three-quarter-length trousers. In most cases they wore long black stockings and boots; no bare knees were to be seen, though one or two boys had bare feet.

23   1914: Tweeds and boater, business suit, shooting coat

One effect of social change was very obvious at that time. During the later years of the nineteenth century the nation became sport-conscious, so that sporting clothes became common wear for everyday affairs. In the most fashionable circles a short-jacket tweed suit was accepted as normal. Before the sporting era, the wealthier classes were marked out by clothes unsuitable for working, and a gentleman only wore at the hunt an outfit suitable for field activity. When the change began, lord and labourer wore the tweed jacket in the country so that the market in tweed increased, and with it that of informal hats. Thus by 1914 anyone might be wearing tweeds—the greatest social leveller ever seen up to that date.

Possibly the 'up-grading' from below came about by means of the reduction in prices through improved manufacture, which made it easier for workers to get respectable clothing. Education had developed self-respect, so that lower-income people tended to adopt prevailing fashions where possible—at least in the towns. There were few workers who did not possess Sunday dress of the same style as their employers. This applied to women as well as men, for a clever home dressmaker with a sewing machine could base her output on a fashionable magazine with patterns. Weldon's patterns, in particular, were a great help to poor women in this respect.

During the war years there were no outstanding changes in women's styles; the tunic effect was retained in dresses and suits, and skirt-hems remained at about six inches from the ground. In a picture of a Royal party at Ascot in 1917 most of the women wore light colours, with their coats varying a little in length—10–14 inches below the waist—and well-waisted. Each woman of the party wore a big, light-coloured fox fur slung over one shoulder, usually the left. Wide-brimmed, stiff hats and flat-heeled, white, lace-up shoes completed the attire.

By 1919 the hat-brim was curved to dip on each side, but small brims were very popular. One may see even at that date how doggedly some older women clung to styles a dozen years out of date. In the Royal Pavilion on the steps of the Victoria Memorial, a spectator at the Victory March appeared with the Edwardian reversed-S figure—full bosom balanced by generous rear curves.

Soon after 1920 a revolution was taking place. A fashion writer of 1922 remarked: 'Some moralists object to the closeness with which clothes are made to fit the body, but these critics form only a small minority. The fashion . . . predominates in all smart circles.'

In view of the styles of that time, one can only think that, if the clothes did indeed fit closely to the body, the latter must have been most peculiar. It was an age of neutralised femininity. Old-type corsets that stressed the waist, bosom, and hips were discarded, and a straight, flat line was achieved, with ankle-length skirts. Everything tended to the long line. Any form of sash or girdle was around the hips, to increase the waistless impression; long drape effects descended from the shoulders, and pearls or beads were worn on strings measuring yards.

In the models of the period three main necklines were to be seen —ordinary round types, boat-variations, and a deep plunge line only made wearable by the flat-chested look that women cultivated. Long sleeves were usually in bell form, and a large motif or bow ornamented the hip-level waist. Evening dresses were often very low cut, with the waist at the hips, and one or two designs showed a diagonal wrap-over style from shoulder to hip.

This was the dawn of the artificial age in textiles. Though crêpe-de-chine, ninon, and chiffon were favourite light stuffs, they were to be outstripped by artificial silk, later known as art silk. It was first produced by Count Hilaire de Chardonnet, at Besançon, in 1884; the Count made a glutinous fluid of cellulose and nitrate by putting them into a mixture of alcohol and ether. When it was forced through tiny holes, the fluid became solid through evaporation, and fine threads were formed. There was nothing in common with actual silk, except that the fibre was inflammable. Its nitrate was extracted for safety.

In 1892 another form of thread was made by heating alkali cellulose with carbon bisulphide, which made a less dangerous material. After 1900 Samuel Courtauld took charge of the new product, then called 'rayon' because of its gleaming threads. These man-made fibres were based on cellulose itself, but a further stage was rayon made from the acid of cellulose (acetate rayon). This type of fibre was made in 1920, by the British Celanese Company of Spondon, Derby.

A famous authority on costume once said that women's fashions tended to pin-point different charms in turn. During the mid-1920s most attention was drawn to the legs—a revolutionary move, after centuries of long skirts. By 1925 there was a general shortening to 10 inches or more from the ground. At that time the effect was that of legs beneath a narrow tube; the skirt was straight as well as short, and the flat-chested figure was still the mode. A number of slimming preparations were on sale, with diet and exercise sheets.

Between 1925 and 1927 the hemline was brought to knee-length. This gave prominence to flesh-tinted silk stockings for well-to-do women, and art silk with cotton tops for their imitators on lower incomes. Narrow, pleated skirts preserved the boyish appearance, which was accentuated by the hairstyle. Short hair, the wartime factory girl's necessity, had become fashionable in the 1920 bob.

For many women the new style was relief from a burden. Long hair, however beautiful, was a mixed blessing—difficult to keep tidy, a labour to wash and dry, and a tyrant of a hundred brush

Edwardian roll

1914   Factory bob   'Listening in' 1923   Shingle 1924   Bingle

Eton crop 1928   Page-boy bob, 1930   1940 Styles

No-perm roll 1942   Pompadour   1964   Pony-tail   1967-68 Curtain

24   Hairstyles: changing fashions

strokes per night. For the first two or three years, though, many a domestic storm blew up when wife or daughter brought her shorn head before the family circle. Male disapproval was widespread, but it passed; short hair became so familiar that variations appeared in 1925. A graduated clipping at the back of the head, leaving the sides puffed, was called a 'shingle', and there was a lesser version, combining bob and shingle, which was called a 'bingle'. One long-hair style reflected the newly introduced broadcasting service (1921). A plait was coiled over each ear in imitation of the head-phones used with early radio sets; this was called the 'listening-in' hairstyle (24).

These efforts to streamline hairdressing reached their peak in the Eton crop of 1927—a completely mannish haircut. This looked extremely smart for the right woman, especially a blonde, but the features had to be near-perfect to carry off such a cold, severe style. Eton crops went hatless, but this was a period of distinctive hats, like the cloche (bell) type (25). Its name was appropriate, for this narrow, deep-crowned hat could be pulled right down over the

61

1922

Cloche
1924

1934

1946

Halo, 1946

1968
Turban

25   Hats: changing styles

head to the eyebrows. Some extreme cloches were so tight as to muffle the wearer's hearing. Naturally the hat could only be worn over a short hairstyle, but the other small type, the round, flat, brimless toque, would set on long hair. Queen Mary always wore a toque.

There was a great craze for leather boots in 1926. These were styled 'Russian boots', and they reached to about five or six inches below the knee, with a sling-strap at the back. It was a brief though intensive fashion cult: only a year later there was scarcely a pair to be seen.

A feature of the 1927–9 period was the wrap-over coat, with a long sweep to fasten on a single huge button over the left hip. Frequently the long rever was rolled with fur up to a deep collar. Fur trimming was applied to hem and cuffs, and some coats had a stole effect with fur at the ends(26). Smart women wore high-heeled court shoes of a light colour in town, with low lace-ups for walking.

It is significant that women no longer adorned themselves as tender violets, inviting, but shrinking from the male regard; they commanded attention by their appearance and forthrightness. Women considered it smart to display a cigarette-case, and a long holder (though small, dainty 'ladies' cigarettes' were on sale), and the sophisticated woman had a make-up outfit in her underarm handbag. In the 'compact' was powder and a pad, with lipstick, and a mirror in the lid.

Quite frequently women could be seen applying powder and lipstick in public, though rouge and eye make-up (mascara) were usually dealt with privately. Many women plucked their eyebrows to a high, thin arch, and underwent some discomfort to keep the line.

While this feminine self-assertion was going on, men's clothes were showing a marked change. In the first place, the die-hard suit was giving way to 'separates', for casual wear—grey flannel trousers, with tweed sports jackets, and Fair Isle pullovers came into common use. Plus-fours, like baggy knickerbockers, were adapted from the golf course for everyday wear. After many years of relatively narrow trousers, the flamboyant male broke out into 'Oxford bags' in 1924—wide, flapping flannels, 25 inches or more around the bottom. These were heaven-sent for cartoonists, and the joke sections of newspapers and magazines were full of parachuting wearers of Oxford bags (*26*). One joke artist showed a bewildered child, unable to reach his mother's short skirts for refuge, but hiding himself in the folds of his father's trousers.

Among young bloods it was the fashion to wear a very short, dark, double-breasted coat, tightly waisted with or without built-in corsets, and wide silver-grey flannels, with sharply pointed shoes. Though stiff collars were still much worn, the up-to-date casual shirt had two soft collars with bone stiffeners for the ends, and tabs that secured the ends to the collar-stud, under the tie-knot. These tabs were often hard to get on to the stud, for the latter already had two ends of the shirt neckband and two of the inside

26   1922 (*left*), 1925–7 (*right*). Men's and women's clothes in the 1920s

bands of the collar threaded upon it. For this reason, a kindly stud-maker produced a stud the top of which was snapped into the stem of the stud, instead of the usual hinged top. A drawback was that if the wearer was doing something strenuous, the strain might cause the stud-top to pop out and disappear, leaving shirt and collar adrift.

Apart from the swing away from formality, the 1920s was a period when the public became increasingly aware of the outdoors, especially the seaside. Before the war, bathing costumes had still been fancy dress, like Victorian types(27): even the men's were like weird combinations in bed-tick stripes. By 1928, all that was gone: cotton swimsuits of reasonable size and shape were available for both sexes, and woollen patterns were increasingly popular. A healthy exposure to sea and sun became the recognised summer weekend tonic by 1930, and hardy individuals with shorts and packs tramped the uncongested roads of the day.

Continental 'beach wear' seized the fancy of Englishwomen. In

27   Swimsuit, early 1900s

1930 'beach pyjamas', with wide flapping trousers, became the rage, and they remained in fashion for several years. Despite this, masculine styles in general were abandoned by women during the next year or so. Both skirts and hair became considerably longer; soft waved styles of hair were worn (the permanent wave was well established), and femininity returned to the woman's world.

One handy invention had been developed for general use by 1925—the zip-fastener, which abolished the ancient tyranny of hook-and-eye. This ingenious system had been produced before the war by the Swedish doctor Gideon Sundback and his Jewish father-in-law Aronson, but it was slow to gain public favour. It was only when the zip-fastener was featured at the Wembley Exhibition of 1924 that it caught the visitors' attention, and from then on it became the rage of Europe and America.

As if to check the feminine trend, slacks became the accepted casual wear for women, and some outdoor types wore shorts after 1930. In fact, the increasing cult of sun worship brought special 'sun-suits', usually made up of brassière-top, shorts, and coatee, in gay patterns. During that decade, the cult of the beach drew more attention to swimsuits, and the two-piece in wool was popular by 1935.

Throughout the period 1930–9 the accent was on soft and sweeping lines, though towards the end of the decade there was a considerable shortening of the skirt. A number of pleasing long-hair styles were favoured, such as the page-boy bob with its under-turned ends. Most hats were almost crownless, and were tipped over one eye, but some extremely smart pill-box shapes were worn, with an elastic band under the hair at the back. About 1937 the 'snood' became fashionable, a caul or veil of heavy net, and many women went entirely hatless, with a scarf at hand for emergency.

After the heady era of Oxford bags, men's trousers were cut in a more restrained style, though rather wider than in the pre-Oxford period. Men were breaking away from a number of tyrannies that had oppressed them for years. Braces were abandoned, by young men at least, and sock suspenders followed—men just let their socks wrinkle, and were free of restriction. For some time the old-style long pants had been going out of use, and short or legless trunks were worn instead. Some forms of semi-stiff collar, which kept their shape without starch, were available on collar-attached shirts. Those wretched little tabs on collars had gone, and the maddening collar-stud was usually replaced by a button.

American coat-style shirts, to be put on like a coat and buttoned up, appeared in England about 1925, but the old-type, over-the-head shirt continued in use for another 10 years, until coat-shirts became common. In sports shirts a cellular material was used, which was honeycombed with tiny holes for coolness.

With the rationing of clothes by coupons during the Second World War, a severe restraint was put upon buying by either sex. Women went stockingless as much as possible, for each pair took a coupon. A man's suit took 35 coupons. Less attention was paid to the price than to the number of coupons required for an article, and shopkeepers spent dreary evenings counting their little pieces of paper to make their returns. 'Utility' was the trademark on wartime clothes, with a curious astronomical-looking symbol. Under such circumstances there could be little variation in styles, particularly as Paris designers were in an occupied country, and out of touch with Britain. It was pleasing to see the superior cut of utility clothes when they were produced by firms like Simpsons of Piccadilly, as compared with the general standard.

For women the war years were a period of uniforms, overalls, and 'sensible' dress, with skirts a shade below the knee, and a square-shouldered cut to the coats. This, of course, was a military reflection. There was a great move towards slacks, largely for practical reasons; some women wore complete man-style suits. However, when peace came, a counter-move reversed the trend; mannish dress was entirely out, and a most interesting revival of some Victorian features came about.

In the most extreme of these 1947 styles, paradoxically called the 'New Look', appeared once more the sloping shoulders and hand-span waists. Naturally the hat was small, a flat little flower-decked creation complete with veil, and the hair was drawn back to form a high coil on which the hat was tilted. A rather unbecoming mid-calf skirt length competed with an ankle-length hobble skirt, slit at the side in the manner of 1910. Above the latter was worn a tightly waisted short coat with a 'peplum' giving a tunic effect, and a military-style 'plastron' or coat-front with large buttons. This *ensemble* was crowned by a flat hat with large flowers, which was perched up sideways on a drawn-back hairstyle featuring the chignon—another Victorian note(28).

Perhaps the most spectacular aid to fashion designers of the post-1945 period was the commercialising of man-made fibres on a large scale. Nylon was actually developed some years before the war, being based on the discoveries of Dr W. H. Carothers in the American laboratories of E. I. Pont de Nemoirs. This material is a synthetic resin, prepared by melting the substance and forcing it through tiny holes, as with rayon. Like many new products, it had its teething troubles, though nylon stockings were a tremendous success from the outset. Women grumbled about the early nylon garments as being non-absorbent and too transparent. Constant experiment and improvement had ruled out these defects

New Look, 1947
Sling-back, wedge-heel shoes

Peep-toe shoes

Long line, 1951

1953
Tulip
Line

H-Line, 1954

A-Line, 1955

28   From the 'New Look' to the 'A-Line'

by 1956, and there was a continual flow of new nylon fabrics for clothes, bedclothes, and upholstery fabric.

While nylon was advancing, the first British synthetic fibre, Terylene, was being developed by John Whinfield (1901–66) in association with Dr T. E. Dickson. Whinfield invented Terylene in 1941, at the works of the Calico Printers' Association, in Lancashire. It was declared a secret by the wartime Ministry of Supply, and it did not come on the market until 1955.

These two amazing fabrics, in mixtures or with a proportion of natural fibres, are the bases of the present-day textile trade, with a vast range of uses. A boon to the housewife—and the bachelor— are the drip-dry, non-iron Bri-Nylon and Terylene shirts, the 'indestructible' stretch Bri-Nylon socks, and the nylon sheets that can be washed, dried, and re-used in a day.

Bri-Nylon socks are especially useful in being truly self-supporting; there had been many previous attempts to gain this comfort, with constricting elasticated socks. Terylene is a boon in that trousers of this material can be soaked with rain, and yet they will dry in the space of an hour without showing a sign of ill-effect. In actual rainwear a useful material is P.V.C., a form of rubberised plastic which does not split easily and does not develop condensation inside.

During the fashion revolution of the 1950s 'lines' followed one another with great regularity. First came the wasp-waist long line in 1951, where the waist was inches lower than that of the new look, and the skirt was widely flared. Two years later the tulip line showed a short, bell-like skirt, still with the tiny waist, but the 1954 H-line gave the waist much less emphasis. It achieved a flat-chested look, while the skirt was a forerunner of the later 'pencil skirt'. This style was followed in 1955 by the A-line, with a curious triangular appearance aided by a diagonal wrap-over in the coat (28). There was a hemline war in 1956, when designers competed for support of the longer or shorter skirt, but there was little doubt of a short-skirt victory.

A very pleasing form was popular in 1960—a stiffened short skirt, like an inverted flower, which gave a charming effect to floral summer frocks. On the other hand, there was an increasing trend for slacks and 'trews'—tight-fitting trousers, which developed straps under the instep in 1961. These were often worn with huge 'Sloppy Joe' jumpers or jackets like the early Victorian 'paletots' and free-flying long hair.

Between 1955 and 1968, women's clothes were wildly varied. At the one extreme, the chic tailored suit or the floral frock; at the other, a baggy, shapeless top of some kind, faded blue overalls called jeans, and long, strappy hair. It was sometimes difficult to distinguish boy from girl among a crowd of adolescents when long-hair fashions became the rage with young men in the mid-1960s. It was most interesting to see the styles that had flourished 100 years before, especially when these were allied with beards or long, bushy sidewhiskers.

This excessive growth of hair was one of the later stages of the 'early-twentieth-century' cult among young men. American-style 'zoot suits', with immensely long, wide-shouldered, draped jackets, were the introductory stage. This led into an 'Edwardian' phase, involving tight trousers, high-cut coats, and narrow string ties, while the shoes were big, yellow affairs with immensely thick soles (34). By 1961, these had given place to 'winkle-pickers', narrow shoes with long, sharp toes.

CHANGES IN FASHION

29 Young people's fashions, 1967–8

While older people continued their sober round of everyday styles, the accent upon those for young people became even more marked in the outfitting trade. In 1962 the 'Beatle suit', in black, with a round-neck, collarless coat, was the smart young man's wear, but within a year or two this had given place to separates, a loose top with tight trousers or jeans. High, black-leather boots often formed part of this outfit. One youth confessed to the author that it took him 20 minutes to get into each leg of his trousers.

Long trousers came into universal use by toddlers and growing boys. They were fitted up as soon as they could walk, and they grew up in them. Rarely did a boy appear in shorts for everyday wear.

Any male freaks of fashion were far outclassed by the extreme shortness of the skirt styles from 1966 onward. A special name, the 'mini-skirt' was coined for those that scarcely appeared to be skirts at all. Hemlines six or eight inches above the knee became common, and in some designs the skirt was skin-tight as well (29). For some years previously, during cold weather, women had worn 'tights' (pantee stockings), and these were now developed in sheer nylon for everyday wear with mini-skirts. Long leather boots sometimes formed part of this attire, but light, stiletto-heeled shoes were general.

On the beach, sun-and-sea outfits were extraordinarily scanty. Since the middle 1950s, the 'bikini' had been worn, becoming more and more revealing (30). This style gained its name from Bikini Atoll, in the Pacific, where the first hydrogen bomb was exploded; the reference was to the bikini's shattering effect.

An interesting revival in the middle of the 1960s was the high hairstyle. By means of pads and back-combing, women achieved

30   Bikini

an appearance very much like that of 200 years before. It was very bad for the hair, as back-combing tended to split and weaken it. As bleaching and tinting were done a great deal, the effect on the hair was harmful.

The mini-skirts of 1967 were allied to a new floral cult, featuring flower-patterned dresses, tinkling bells on chains around the neck, and immensely long, flowing hair. This floral aspect also appeared in the clothes of young men: both sexes wore complete trouser suits in floral style, and flowers in the hair. An extreme group of young men emulated women in back-combing, bleaching or dyeing their hair, and many had regular permanent waving.

A final note on fashion trends concerns woman's enemy, the advancing years. Cosmetic surgery had been developed to an amazing degree in repairing faces shattered by war, and after the war the art came to be applied in the beauty parlour. Faces that had begun to sag and wrinkle were subjects for the surgeon's skill. In the best treatment, he removed fat from under the skin to produce tautness and pull out wrinkles.

Usually, cosmetic surgery was applied to the nose, the skin around the eyes, the facial lines, and the neck, the nose being the most frequently treated. Eyelines were usually the first target for treatment regarding wrinkles, and their removal could take up to

70

15 years off the subject's age. It was important, though, that she should be no older than 40 for the best results; if the lines were deep, it was difficult to eliminate them completely. A normal charge for a 'facial' in 1968 might be up to £300, with the prospect of a repeat in about five years.

Popular lesser beauty aids of this period were false eyelashes and fingernails. A number of women used a 'hair piece', which could cost £30 or more but helped them to vary their hairstyle.

Chapter V

THE JUVENILE REVOLUTION

IF we survey the condition of children in general at the time of the First World War, we find them almost entirely subject to their surroundings. Among the wealthier classes, the Victorian attitude survived—rigid upbringing, an obsession with class codes, and a fixed pattern of behaviour. Though this repressive system has been strongly criticised, it did tend to foster a regard for courtesy and the elements of gracious living. It brought a type of inbred gentility that smoothed relations between humans in a manner that can still be seen occasionally. At this end of the scale was the range of graceful accomplishments, the recitation and the musical performance, the deference to parents and teachers, which marked the child of good home background.

A level of childhood conduct such as was seen in a well-to-do household was the aim of various poorer grades, all striving to reach the level above. This served to bring up a considerable number of children in the ruling-class tradition of a 'decent' mode of life and conduct. Unless we realise this, it is easy to over-simplify early-twentieth-century life into rags and riches, without any intermediary stages.

Children were then, as now, like plants, dependent upon the soil that bore them, the nourishment they received, the protection that was accorded them. In good soil and well tended, they could grow up strong and healthy. If their roots were in poor soil, and no care was taken to nurture their growth, it was a different story. A stunted, perhaps deformed plant, sickly and wind-battered, struggling for its too-short life, and never knowing the delight of healthy growth. In the same way, the mental outlook could be warped by evil influences and lack of training in the everyday decencies.

That was a period of father-son and mother-daughter relationships among the self-respecting workers, where the growing sons followed the training of the father in the everyday tasks done by the man of the house. In the garden, in the shed with some piece of carpentry, clearing the roof-gutters—each boy with his tasks, and the satisfaction of doing them well. Meanwhile, the girls were gathering a knowledge of woman's work in the kitchen, at the serving table, or in cleaning the house. They might be 17 before they dressed in long skirts and put their hair up as a sign that they were to be considered as young women.

Similarly, the boys wore knickerbockers or curious long shorts over black stockings until they left the elementary school at 14; then, amid derisive howls from their younger associates, they appeared in long trousers. This ordeal was not for boys of well-to-do parents, whose sons were betrousered at a relatively early age for the public schools.

In the absence of ready-made amusements, country children were thrown back on their own devices, and through this there flourished the rural crafts, wood-carving, rush baskets, and needlewomen's arts. Town-dwellers' families had more public amusements provided for them, but there was still a good deal of home entertainment in games, music, and the 'cutting-out' and 'sticking-on' pastimes.

In the great-city slums, a sickening state of affairs existed in 1914. Here the old-time disregard of children, the attitude that they were miserable nuisances still prevailed, and like neglected animals many thousands of them clung to hopeless life. In those dark, fever-ridden alleys, rank with filth and vermin, the precious young lives struggled for survival. Children whose heads were scratched raw through lice, children whose revolting clothes had not been off their pitiful skeleton bodies for six months, children with suppurating eyes—deformed through neglect, unwanted, beaten

31 Slum child and school nurse—
from a photograph of 1908

73

heartlessly—there was desperate misery in all city slum areas.

An example of devoted rescue and unflagging courage in the cause of childhood was the great Scotswoman, Margaret MacMillan. We shall consider her nursery school in the next chapter but this was only part of her magnificent service to the slum children of Bradford. She was the only woman on the Bradford School Board, and its youngest member, but her activities revealed and did much to remedy the miseries of poor children. Our chapter on education will show how Miss MacMillan's tireless campaigning brought school clinics, nurses, dental treatment, and baths for Bradford children long before the First World War.

32 Boys and girls of 1914 from contemporary photographs

More widespread still were the efforts of Thomas John Barnardo (1845–1905), the great Irish doctor whose children's homes have been a byword for a century. Dr Barnardo opened his first home for destitute children at Stepney Causeway, in London's East End, and that building is still the headquarters of a network of rescue centres. Before the kindly doctor died, over 100 of his homes had been established, while a family of 60,000 children had found new life there, and entered the grown-up world as useful citizens.

This was the most famous of the child-rescue organisations, but noble work was also done by other homes, and by the Salvation Army. It was a means of relieving the misery of neglected children, but this did not educate their parents in tenderness and child care —that was to remain a problem for many years.

Among the private efforts to band young people together in some form of communal activity, the Girls' Friendly Society takes a deservedly high place. It was founded in 1875, and by 1902 there were 150,000 members, gathering to receive instruction and exchange ideas on domestic arts, as well as on outdoor recreation. This society was an admirable centre for girls in domestic service and factory workers in the towns, while for country girls it provided pleasant social contacts that they certainly would not have had otherwise.

Boys had the military-style Boys' Brigade, a religious organisation founded by Sir William Smith of Glasgow in 1883. Each company was affiliated to a local church, and the boys looked smart on parade with their pipeclayed belts and jaunty caps. A rousing bugle band was a great feature of the Brigade's public appearances.

Certainly the most famous boys' unit was Sir Robert Baden-Powell's Boy Scouts, based on the boys of Ladysmith who made themselves so useful as messengers when the town was besieged by the Boers in 1899. In 1907 the first camp of the movement, with 24 boys, was established on Brownsea Island, in Poole Harbour, Dorset. These lads, in their shorts, their broad-brimmed hats and bush shirts, with broad neckerchiefs that could be used as slings, were to become a byword in public service. Junior Scouts formed units of Cubs, and the keynote of the whole was self-reliance, especially in outdoor activities.

Not to be outdone, girls formed a similar organisation of their own—the Girl Guides, a movement founded by Agnes Baden-Powell, with the help of her brother, Sir Robert, in 1910(*33*). Guides did public service, like the Scouts, but they added homecraft and child care. They were divided into three age groups—Brownies, 7–11; Guides, 11–16; and

33 Girl Guides: uniform changes, 1910, 1948, 1965

Rangers, 16–21. Both boys and girls were trained in first aid and signalling; for this and various other pursuits proficiency badges were awarded.

At the end of the First World War a problem was presented by the number of adolescents who were finding mischief in idleness. In spite of the good work by religious associations in providing recreational centres, there was much wilful and mischievous conduct by youths in their middle teens. This arose from the lack of restraint in the absence of so many fathers. Soon the state of affairs was noticed in official circles, so that a shadowy Government connection was maintained.

By 1930, there was definite State interest in what had come to be called 'the service of youth', and the Board of Education circular 1486 declared its responsibility for youthful welfare. In each case the concern was with social contacts, education in codes of conduct, physical training, and recreation.

When the Board's circular appeared, its contents showed the three-way linking of interested bodies—the Government as a whole, the local education authority, and those welfare movements that were already concerned with the young. Through this interlinking came the phrase 'youth service', to be maintained from that time. Having been accepted as a part of education, the service was in need of regular teachers, so courses for full-time or part-time youth leaders were arranged after the 1944 Act. This passed to local authorities the matter of youth training, and as the county college was a proposal of the Act there seemed to be great possibilities.

In spite of such a good start, the youth movement suffered a great setback after 1945. There was less enthusiasm for it in the new ministry—new schools and technology took first place. Thus hundreds of unofficial youth leaders, inspired by the work, were left to struggle against crumbling buildings, inadequate kit, and, often, indifferent youngsters. That was one of the burdens of the undertaking—the leader's work was so often sacrificed to the heedless. This was not altogether the fault of the young ones. They had come through an upheaval, their formative years spent in an atmosphere of danger, terror, and shortages. It was to be seen in the later generation of adolescents, those born during or soon after the struggle, for their mothers passed to them some of the strain and anxiety of the war years.

THE JUVENILE REVOLUTION

In the mid-1950s a new adolescent was beginning to emerge. There was an increasingly adult outlook among children barely in their teens, the reflection of their birth conditions. Another most important factor was the working mother; as the child could not go home during the day, he was thrown back on his own resources, with toughening results. Similarly, the fact that his mother was not available until the evening made her image of less consequence, and this added to the independent spirit.

Undoubtedly there was a powerful American influence at work in the early 1950s. Their expression 'teenager' was adopted, and the parent-child relationship of America was reflected through the presence of many American troops. In addition, the craze for Rock'n'roll had a tremendous effect. Bill Haley and his Comets, with their off-beat rhythm, completely captivated the young, and 'rock' swept the country like a storm. Wherever young people gathered, it only needed that insistent thud—thud to set them clapping and swaying like automata.

In great-city cinemas, where 'Rock around the Clock' was showing, there were high-spirited teenagers 'rocking' in the aisles. It brought quite serious disturbances, not so much evil as over-excited, so that cinema managers behaved warily. At one showing attended by the author in a provincial cinema, the younger members of the audience began the slow clap. At once the volume was reduced, so that the beat was less exciting.

34 Edwardian ('Teddy-boy') style

This enthusiasm, and the great sales of 'rock' records, confirmed the growth of a new type of youngster. For some years the departure was expressed in music, but near the end of the decade the 'Edwardian' craze set in, and the next stage of the juvenile take-over had begun (34). An Edwardian urge affected girls as well, so that 'Teddy-girls' were to be seen gyrating

77

with 'Teddy-boys'. Unfortunately some of the latter behaved in a highly objectionable way, causing much annoyance and damage: in some cases personal injury was inflicted on the public. This had the effect of souring the public, and the title 'Teddy-boy' became synonymous with 'trouble-maker'.

Soon afterwards teenagers began the invasion of south-eastern coast resorts, especially Brighton and Clacton. Rival leather-coated gangs, styling themselves 'Mods' and 'Rockers' respectively, descended on the towns in motor-scooter fleets, terrorising the older people. Urged on by their girl companions, the gangs fought pitched battles on the beaches and in the streets. These young nuisances drew much attention, like those whose destructive instincts led them to wreck youth clubs and public places. However, it was not among them that the development of juveniles was to be seen. For every irresponsible rioter, there were hundreds of decent, well-behaved boys and girls.

It was obvious that girls developed a mature outlook more quickly than boys, and by the mid-1960s this was plain in the girls' choice of male company. Girls of 15 preferred young men of 18 or 20, while 15-year-old boys seemed to go out with girls of 13. These girls, even at that age, were well accustomed to permanent waves, make-up, high heels, and nylons. Many parents found themselves amiably overruled by their children so that the household became one of equals instead of a directed family.

Amid the economic uplift that workers experienced at that time, adolescents were receiving wages previously unheard-of for people of their age. Of course, they were the target of traders, for it was said quite seriously that teenagers were the *nouveaux riches*. Many had perhaps £10 a week or more and no responsibilities—many of them paid only token sums at home—and often the whole amount would be spent on pay-day. Bizarre clothes, records, dances, and coffee bars were the usual money drains, but often a motor-cycle or car had to be maintained.

A high-powered sales campaign was concentrated on teenagers from all directions, so that they vied with each other to be 'with it'. They were horrified at the thought of being a 'square', i.e. one whose outlook and tastes were 'old-fashioned'.

It was clear that a great cleavage existed between adolescents and adults, even in 1962; the young ones were in a separate world which grown-ups could not enter. Youth club leaders were tolerated, but excluded. In the Beatle age, which began in 1962, the watch-word was 'beat'—beat music, beat dance, and beat singer. One had only to look in on a beat dance to see how remote the teen-agers' world was from anything that older people had known in their youth. A darkened hall, the only subdued light coming from the stage, where half-a-dozen wildly contorting pop group players twanged, wailed, and drummed. Undulating forms packed the floor, moving slowly on the same spot, the eerie light doing strange things to the girls' faces: an other-world atmosphere that precluded intrusion.

Even the eating habits of the young had completely changed. Where once the sweet things, cakes, jellies, jam, and trifles were unfailingly successful, they were quite out of favour when the beat age dawned. The only acceptable items were savouries—chipolatas and olives on sticks, tiny bacon rolls, cheese, and potato crisps. An invitation to tea was hopelessly square; in fact, visits or parties always implied snack feeding rather than a sit-down. For that reason, Wimpy bars and snack bars were favoured before restaurant or café, and hamburgers with coffee rather than 'roast with two veg'.

Those parents who took the broadest view of their children's outlook cooperated amazingly when a party was planned. Having put ready refreshment, the parents retired to one room, and gave over the house to the young people, regardless of swing records, wild twangings, and wilder shrieks.

During the period 1963-4, shrieks were at their most piercing. Whenever teenagers' music idols appeared in public—the Beatles, the Rolling Stones, and similar star entertainers—there were hysterical scenes (35). Most of the frenzy came from the girls, some barely in their teens. For instance, when the Beatles were due in at London Airport, it was a major operation to keep the girls at bay. They pulled their long hair down over their faces and screamed wildly; they swarmed on passenger-bay roofs, and tested the bar-riers to the utmost. As the Beatles' car was crawling through the seething crowd, girls were beating on the roof and windows, or sprawling over the bonnet. When the four young men were on stage, the volume of the girls' screaming was only matched by their endurance in keeping it up. More than once a performance was completely ruined by screaming.

That phase passed, so that by 1965 the mass hysteria was less in evidence. There was still the flamboyant dress, the brass-studded

35   The audience listening to a performance by the Rolling Stones

black leather, and the high boots. Not so much was heard of the 'ton-up' boys, who had done a 'ton' (100 m.p.h.) on their motor-cycles.

At that time a new term was current in the entertainment world of the young—the 'discotheque'. For some years records, known as discs, had been popular in conjunction with the self-changing record player. A radio announcer who ran a record programme was styled a 'disc jockey' and the discotheque was a place of enter-tainment with music from discs. In collecting these discs, many adolescents became connoisseurs of contemporary music. A famous newspaper had a panel of four young people to contribute reviews on the arts appropriate to their age group.

Wondering parents compared notes on the vagaries of their young. Here the son had filled his bedroom with collector's oddities—carriage lamps, old destination boards, pseudo-antiques specially made for sale to teenagers. Perhaps the 16-year-old daughter was frantically wishing for a 'hair-piece' or switch, such as women of 30 were wearing. It was widely agreed that the 'with-it' young of the late 1960s were a mystery to their parents.

Even the very young displayed a shrewd self-possession entirely at odds with tradition. A good instance was sent to a London newspaper by a young mother. After buying a projector to show films that had been taken on holiday, the mother found it to be defective. When her daughter, aged six, came home from school eager to see the films, the news had to be broken. With diffidence the mother began:

'The projector——'

'Don't tell me!', broke in the child. 'It doesn't work!'

'However did you know?'

'Nothing *ever* works!'

This worldly-wise outlook was common among young people of all ages. In school, the teacher was able to discuss features of the lesson through intelligent questions from the class. Physical well-being matched the developed mind. Those who had witnessed a gathering of children 50 years before could not fail to be impressed by the standard of health among the lively young ones of the 1960s. School meals, however much criticised, and the school milk issue had played a great part in building up child health. Some authorities believed that these factors brought about the early maturity of the schoolgirls of that time, though the boys did not display the same effects.

Among town schoolboys, at least, it was quite the normal thing to be doing part-time employment, and this helped the mature outlook. By earning money—£3 a week or more, in some cases—the boys felt a measure of independence. They could buy clothes, and contribute to their keep, and they had no need to ask their parents for pocket money. All this tended to promote a self-confident, adult outlook.

Early in 1967 England became aware of a new interest among the young. Mini-skirts and long, curtain-like hair were familiar enough, but there was a different pattern in dress material—a whirling fantasia of floral design.

36 Flower people. 1967

81

Attention was drawn more particularly by the tinkling bells slung around the necks, and by long ropes of beads, large and small.

In the long hair was fastened a flower, and this was the symbol—these were the 'flower people' or 'hippies', a new cult of unusual outlook(36). Their declared policy was one of love and peace—in fact, the slogan 'Make love, not war,' appeared over their gatherings. Another symbol of the flower people was the practice of going barefoot. They sometimes used the phrase 'flower power' as propaganda: their expressed belief was that, if violence were met with a gift of a flower, it could be turned aside. Male hippies wore floral suits, though they do not seem to have gone barefoot so frequently.

Some strange news items of 1967 brought young people to the fore. A 10-year-old girl, Beverley Williams, of Ruislip, was chosen to represent Britain as a high diver in an Anglo-American swimming contest. In the local court, an application was made by a girl of 14, through her father, for an injunction to stop teenage girl neighbours from persecuting her.

Throughout the 1960s there was a heavy stress on the needs of youth, with the term applied to a wide range of activities: youth hostels, youth employment officers, the Youth Service Development Council and its monthly magazine, *Youth Service*. In Leicester was opened the National College for the Training of Youth Leaders, and courses were offered in Birmingham and Swansea. Never had there been such an era of opportunity for the young, in the way of openings, grants, and advice. If a suitable training-place for the chosen trade was not available in the district, an assisted apprenticeship scheme helped the candidate's transfer to a town with suitable centres. Lodgings were found and vetted, and grants were available for necessities. This was the age of youth—unheard-of freedom, a plentiful money supply, and exciting opportunity.

Chapter VI
EXPANSION IN EDUCATION

IN 1914 there were wide differences between the various kinds of schools. Children of the numerous poor, in town or country, were attending, in most cases, schools set up by the Local Education Boards of 1870—grey, stone buildings with a strong church influence in the style. This was a reflection of the designs used by the pre-1870 Church of England National Society and the British and Foreign Schools Society.

At least the 1914 children were attending school without fee-paying—the original 1870 system of coppers to defray expenses had been abolished in 1891, except for some higher elementary grades. There was some hope, too, that after 40 years of State-run schools, the children's parents were enlightened enough to encourage them in learning.

It was the Parliamentary Reform Act of 1867 that introduced this system. Under the Act, the vote was greatly extended, to cover all town householders, lodgers in such houses who were paying not less than £10 a year in rent, and countrymen who paid a minimum of £12 rates. It was wisely decided that education was necessary for the sensible use of the vote, and though it was too late to educate the men of voting age in 1867, at least provision could be made for the rising generation. Three men were responsible for the bill that opened the school doors—Henry A. Bruce (later Lord Aberdare), W. E. Forster, and Algernon Egerton. Their bill of 1867–8 was the basis of the great Education Act, passed in 1870.

There were two main rulings in the Act—a dual system of education, voluntary schools and local authority schools, and strictly unbiased religious instruction. Though at first the locally elected school boards could use their own judgement on compulsory attendance, in 1880 this was enforced throughout England and Wales. Voluntary schools continued on under private management but with State aid and inspectors, while new local, rate-supported schools were created. When the local school board was set up, each elector had as many votes as there were candidates for the

37   Classroom in 1914

board, and he could 'plump', i.e. give all his votes to one man if he wished. After a great deal of discussion on religious instruction, it was decided that the Apostle's Creed should be included, as being common to all beliefs.

School is such an accepted feature of life that it is hard to imagine its impact on the children of 1870. Hundreds of thousands of workers' children had run wild in the streets, or had been put to unsuitable work between the ages of five and 11. After that date, in most areas the schoolroom claimed them, and with them a weekly fee ranging from a penny to eightpence according to the school. In full employment areas the local board might fix the higher rate, though the term 'elementary' could only apply to a school whose fees did not exceed ninepence a week. Where several children of one family were attending school, the 'school pence' were a serious drain on an income of perhaps 15 shillings a week. This led to evasion, as the parents not only lost the children's labour but were forced to pay for their education as well. In cases of real hardship the fees were paid by the local Board of Guardians, but not without a struggle.

In 1880 Mundella's Act provided for district by-laws to enforce school attendance, and from that date school records describe action in this respect:

> 28th August 1885: Joseph Bond summoned before the magistrates for irregularity.
>
> 13th May 1887: Ernest Sanders has played the truant all the week, threatened to be sent to an Industrial School by the School Board.

This referred to the earliest form of approved school for troublesome children. Originally industrial schools were for vagrant children as well as the refractory, under Acts passed between 1857 and 1864. They were for those under 14, who could be kept in the school until they were 16. Senior schools for the purpose were called reformatories, to take youths up to 16 who could be kept until they were 19: these correspond to present-day approved schools (i.e. approved by the Home Office). Master Sanders would have come under the 1876 Education Act, which provided short-term industrial schools for truants.

Every year an examination of schools receiving grants was conducted by inspectors, and results were graded in standards, I to VI (extended to VII in 1882). Reading, writing, and arithmetic were tested, the 'standard' being the accepted level for each age group. There was movement up or down according to ability. On the results of the tests depended the school's grant; the number of passes in each subject were judged for the grant in that subject.

Though the teachers' salaries did not always depend upon the passes (the 'payment by results' system) they frequently received a proportion of the grant, so they tended to urge on the pupils by all available means. In the log-book of one North Devon school (Newport National School, now non-existent), entries like these appear:

> 16th January 1891: Agreed to give the (head) master one quarter of the Gov. Grant in addition to his fixed salary.
>
> 11th November 1898: Form 17A (VS). Grant of £45 was approved, expended as follows: Head Teachers' salaries (man and wife) £20: Assistant Teacher £5. (Remainder on books and furniture.)

An extract from the inspector's report:

> 6th December 1889: I have recommended the payment of the higher grant for both English and Geography though with some hesitation.

Greater dissatisfaction was recorded by the same inspector on 11 January 1892:

> Both discipline and instruction have fallen off. Reading is inaccurate, unintelligent, and without expression. Arithmetic is weak throughout, but especially in the fourth and sixth Standards. English is so defective in the upper standards that I have some hesitation in recommending the payment of the lower grant, and Geography is a failure. Dictation in the second and fourth Standards needs attention. In other respects the work is fairly satisfactory.

This grant system led to a sustained drilling of classes in the basic subjects, at least, and often in the humanities or so-called 'class' subjects, such as history and geography. Scholars who fell below the required standards might be caned:

> 2nd November 1881: Punished 3 girls for mistakes in dictation.

A common means of teacher training was the employment of 'pupil teachers', who had passed through the elementary school. These served four years' apprenticeship, and were then admitted as teachers under progressive articles, until the peak of first-class certificated teacher might be reached. Pupil teachers were still being trained in this way as late as 1938.

Elementary education was all that most workers' children received, but for the wealthier families of the middle and upper classes, secondary education was available in public schools and grammar schools. Only from these could a student reach university.

No precise definition of a public school seems possible. One authority classed it as an institution, usually a boarding school, for the children of wealthy middle-class families, but this does not make clear the distinction between the public school and any other big boarding school. In the late nineteenth century there were nine large public schools—St Paul's and Merchant Taylors, which were not boarding schools; Winchester, Eton, Harrow, Rugby, Charterhouse, Shrewsbury, and Westminster. All public schools taught classical subjects only, until a commission of inquiry directed by Lord Clarendon in 1861 led to the inclusion of humanities on the syllabus, with more choice for the pupils. Headmasters resented the inquiry, and cooperated very grudgingly.

In 1864 the Schools Inquiry Commission, under Lord Taunton, looked into the organisation of endowed schools, including grammar schools and private schools. Though the pupils came from well-to-do families, the parents often had insufficient education to approve their children's courses. Curriculae were often hidebound and not concerned with humanities.

According to the Commission's findings, three divisions could be made in the secondary pupils—a mainly classical education to 18; a course including classics but with a stress on mathematics and modern studies, to end at 16; and a 'clerk's education', in mathematics and English, for the lower middle class up to 14. These courses would reflect the social level of the pupil.

After the survey, Lord Taunton's Commission recommended the division of the country into provinces, to be governed by the Charity Commission, with inspecting trustees and governing bodies, including parents, for each school. This was not done, but the Endowed Schools Act of 1869 set up a commission to form a new code for government. A most outstanding item was the development of girl's secondary education. This was pioneered by Miss Frances Buss (North London Collegiate School), and Miss Dorothea Beale (Ladies' College, Cheltenham). With Miss Beale's school as an example, the Girls' Public Day School Company was set up in 1872, and by 1900 it had built over 70 schools, to house 7,000 girls.

This work laid the foundations for twentieth-century education. A great figure of the early twentieth century had begun his invaluable work in the previous decade. Sidney Webb, Chairman of the London Technical Education Committee in 1892, founded a scholarship system by which Board School boys and girls aged from 11 to 13 could gain up to five years' higher education through examinations. This idea spread, and the Board of Education Act of 1899 set up a central authority to superintend education. Though this body was not very important, it paved the way for the Education Act of 1902, brought forward as a bill by Arthur (later Lord) Balfour.

The 1902 Act established local education authorities in each county and county borough. There had been over 2,500 of the old school boards, but these were now replaced by 330 local bodies. Both elementary and higher education were covered, and voluntary schools were admitted on the rates. All 'payment by results' was abolished, and a complicated system of grants to local authorities helped to relieve the burden on the rates.

There was much quarrelling about the overall grant of rate aid to voluntary schools of all denominations, and Nonconformists demonstrated against being rated for that purpose. An Act of 1904 provided for Government grants in any areas where ratepayers would not cooperate. Robert Morant, Permanent Secretary to the Board of Education, reorganised that body into elementary, secondary, and technical branches. He increased the number of inspectors in each division, and included more women. Secondary school work was planned on an academic basis, for possible university entry, but this made the course suitable only for the few who would achieve that. When the school certificate and the higher certificate were brought in, the same rigid outlook could be seen.

During Morant's term of office, much more attention was paid to poor children's welfare in school, especially as regards nourishing food. This was one of the great benefits of compulsory education, in that educated people were brought into active contact with a childhood problem. A report of 1884 had stated that in London 40 per cent of the children in one school went without breakfast, while in another nearly a quarter of the total entry were half-starved.

Salvation Army centres provided meals for hungry children at a penny each, and other charitable bodies did the same, while teachers frequently paid for pupils' meals and hot drinks. Most appalling to those in contact with the victims was their quiet, uncomplaining misery, as they sat shivering and empty at their hard school desks. These conditions brought two relieving Acts, in quick succession, under the reorganised educational system.

In 1906 the Provision of Meals Act gave authority, and grants if required, to local bodies providing a meals service. At Bradford, in 1907, was seen the first of those processions so familiar in present-day schools—a line of eager faces with plates borne before them(38). Close upon the Meals Act came the Administrative Provisions Act of 1907, which followed the formation of a Medical Department in the Board of Education. Bradford authorities had provided school medical services from 1893.

Under the 1907 Act the national medical service was only partially effective: it covered elementary schools, but the parents were not obliged to act upon the advice. Still, a growing sense of responsibility brought some cooperation. Part of the service was a check on cleanliness, especially as regards lice. Inspections of heads became a regular part of the school nurse's duties after the 1907 Act(31), and in extreme cases the child's head was shorn. A

38   School meals at Bradford—from a photograph of 1907

wash with an infusion of quassia chips was prescribed for nits
(the eggs of lice).

It was much more difficult to launch a school dental service,
which depended so much on parental cooperation, and which
strove to develop the teeth-cleaning habit among people completely
strange to it. School dental clinics were first established in 1907,
and under the same law local authorities were empowered to
supply children with spectacles.

Among the many provisions of the 1907 Act was the so-called
'free place system' for secondary schools. This supplied schools
with a grant of £5 for every child on the roll between the ages of
12 and 18, but certain conditions were attached. At least 25 per
cent of the school's places were to be allocated to elementary
school pupils, on a scholarship examination like that of the Webb
system. Other rules included the admission of all creeds, and the
inclusion of local authority members in the board of governors.

While these great improvements were being made, fierce controversy was raging over the 'half-time system', under which children
attended school for half the day and worked in mills or factories
for the other half. It was often done in alternate order—school
first for one week, factory first during the next week. This system

was most common in the textile areas, and it was reported in 1891 that nearly half the Lancashire children of 10 or over were working half-time—a total of 50,000 children. On mill mornings they began work at six o'clock. It was a wretched state of affairs, tending to make the child dull in school and stunted in growth.

Another side of the picture was shown in the school record of a Church foundation in Barnstaple, North Devon. There was a lace factory near by, and half-timers from it created great disturbance in the school by their unruly conduct. One headmaster, while struggling to subdue a sturdy half-timer, had his leg broken. Half-time was maintained until May 1911, when a merciful bill stopped it in factories, but not on farms; under that bill the school-leaving age was raised from 12 to 13.

In the same year a new type of post-primary school was set up, first in London and then in Manchester. It was known as the 'central school', with a four-year course (11–15) slanted towards industry and commerce, but no pretence of a vocational training. Actual training classes for industrial or domestic employment were already in being, and in 1913 the Board formed these into junior technical schools. There was an annual grant of £5 per head, and pupils were drawn by selection from elementary schools; free places were available by entrance examination.

A later development was the non-selective central school. This took any 11-year-old who had not gained free entry into the grammar school, and whose parents did not wish to pay the fees. By this means, the 'senior school' came into existence, the fore-runner of the 'secondary modern' of 1944.

There was great difficulty in keeping the country's schools open after the outbreak of war in 1914. Apart from Government requisitioning for billets, many teachers volunteered or were conscripted. Large classes and a preponderance of women teachers were the results. An urgent call was made for retired teachers, married women ex-teachers, and anyone of ability to fill the gaps in the teachers' ranks.

During the early years of the war, the devoted sisters Mac-Millan, Rachel and Margaret, were pursuing their project of the nursery school, the first in England. They had established it in London, at Deptford in 1911, and enlarged premises were granted them in early 1914. All the expenses were borne by the sisters until they contracted to care for the children of munition workers at sevenpence a day. This was in effect a crèche, though the idea was quite new then.

In spite of wartime difficulties, the Government made plans for postwar advance; the appointment in 1916 of Herbert A. L. Fisher (1865–1940) as President of the Board was a good move. Fisher was a historian, and Vice-Chancellor of Sheffield University. His Education Act (1918) stressed the need to provide higher education even when the pupil could not pay.

No child was permitted to leave school under the age of 14, and the last vestige of the half-time system was abolished from July 1922. Child labour was strictly confined within limits for

39   Handicrafts in school, 1914

those of school age. No work in mines, factories, or with street traders was permitted, and no child under 12 could work at all. Weekday hours were restricted to one before school and one after attendance, so newsagents could employ children to deliver papers. Under the 1907 Act, each child was medically inspected on admission to a school, and on leaving it. This had been extended in 1912, to allow treatment, which was made compulsory by 1918.

As teachers had been so few during the war years, it was necessary to offer more attractive salaries in order to staff the postwar schools. After a long discussion a combined committee of local authority and teacher representatives was formed in 1919, under the direction of Lord Burnham. Through the work of the Burnham Committee, a national scale of teachers' salaries was adopted, whereas previously salaries had depended on individual school boards.

A great drive for better handwriting was a feature of the schools of the early 1920s. This had always been a prime target, for good appearance and legibility naturally made the teacher look favourably on the work. In former days the copperplate hand had been

91

the ideal, but its decline since the Victorian era led to the search for a new form. It was found in script, the round, unconnected letters associated with infants' books, and for some years teachers and pupils used that in many schools. Another new idea was the practice of woodwork as a general rule, where previously it had been a centralised subject for which classes often left their own schools.

After 1920, educationalists concentrated more on 'adolescent' education, by which they meant that of children over 11. A report from Sir Henry Hadow, Chairman of the Board's Consultative Committee, was issued in 1926, with some practical ideas. It recommended the abolition of the term 'elementary', and the alteration and extension of the meaning of 'secondary', to include all post-primary schools. In order to separate the new secondary schools from those already in existence, the latter would be grammar schools, and the new foundations 'modern' schools. In those the leaving age would be 14. For this reason it was suggested there should be a change at 11, from primary to grammar school (five-year course) or to the modern school (three-year course).

While these plans were maturing, thousands of children throughout the country were being educated under conditions little better than those of 40 years before. School Board buildings in the traditional church-school style were frequently crowded, their antiquated, ill-ventilated classrooms spreading childish ailments among the closely packed victims. In 1947 an elderly teacher showed the author a classroom like an oubliette, with only one remote window—in the high ceiling. For years he had taught 60 pupils every day in that dungeon. Many schools retained inadequate Victorian toilets—in fact, some country schools were still using earth closets in the late 1940s.

Education, like all national concerns, suffered during the difficult decade 1921–31, for the Committee on National Expenditure (Chairman, Sir Eric Geddes) recommended severe cuts. All educational grants were reduced by a third and teachers' salaries were also lowered—they suffered a further 15 per cent cut in 1929. No new school buildings were allowed, except in urgent cases such as on new housing estates, and an amendment was made in the 1907 Act covering scholarship places in secondary schools. If the parent's income was low, the place was still free, but above a certain income there was a sliding scale of payments. This was a reflection of the means test for unemployed workers at the time.

Two more Hadow reports appeared at the end of that troubled period: they concerned the primary school (1931) and the infant school (1933). In the 1931 report, great stress was laid upon non-rigidity, on activity rather than excessive drilling with knowledge, and on broadening the children's experience. This led up to the project method, a piece of work requiring both practical and academic skill, to be produced as a combined class effort. As it happened some overenthusiastic teachers tended to neglect academics for activity, so a balance had to be achieved. Infant schools should be roomy, well-lit, and airy, said the 1933 report, with light chairs and tables rather than desks. Pastel colours were suggested for the decor.

By 1934 the effects of the slump were easing, so teachers' salary cuts were made up again and it seemed a good time to think of raising the school-leaving age to 15. This was laid down in the Education Act of 1936, with the change date as 1 September 1939, though exemption would be given where 'beneficial employment' was offered at 14.

For grammar and technical schools the Consultative Committee published its report in 1938—the Spens Report, directed by Sir Will Spens, Master of Corpus Christi. In this survey appeared a suggestion that still causes great argument. It concerned the multilateral school (grammar, technical, and modern grades in one unit), so that pupils could move between courses varying in academic standard without change of school. It was decided at the time that such a school would be too large and varied for a single headmaster to manage. However, this concept coupled with the Hadow reports formed the basis of the 1944 Act.

On the very day when the leaving age should have been raised, a great exodus was taking place. Under a voluntary system, children were evacuated from 40 highly populated centres, in view of probable bombing under the threat of war. During the next few days, three-quarters of a million school children and many thousands under age were moved. They were transferred to rural areas, under a scheme devised some months before by the Board of Education and the appropriate ministries.

Though the operation was creditably smooth, some difficulties arose, especially when parents could not be given a guarantee that their children would go to a particular place. Those people who witnessed the waiting crowds of young ones, with their

93

40   Evacuees

haversacks and their little respirators, felt it a dreadful indictment of twentieth-century civilisation that danger should threaten them (*40*).

A very disturbing factor was the amount of unconsidered billeting, where East End children, with little training in cleanly living, were housed with families whose outlook was fastidious. It opened the eyes of the general public to the foul conditions in which so many children lived, and gave impetus to the demand for reform in education and welfare.

Schooling was a major problem; existing buildings were crammed, and all kinds of premises were taken over. Matters were further complicated when parents were allowed to visit the evacuees, and many of the latter wished to return home. As there was no bombing in the winter of 1939, thousands of children left their billets to go home, and created a further problem. Their schools could not be used until air-raid shelters had been provided, so between crowded evacuee schools and disorganised danger area schools the children lost nine months of education. When the heavy bombing began in September 1940, there was another mass departure of children, and once again an educational system had to be organised.

Lord Woolton, as Minister of Food (1940–3), directed the School Meals Service as a large-scale operation, in which the parents paid according to their means. A daily milk ration in one-third-pint bottles was provided. By 1950 2¾ million school dinners and five million daily milk rations were the annual issue. Milk had been charged at a halfpenny a bottle, but the charge was abolished by 1947.

Just as in the First World War, educational reform was being

94

planned while the struggle was still going on. In July 1943 R. A. Butler, President of the Board of Education, issued a White Paper on the subject. This was followed by a bill which became the Education Act of 1944, and which contained some sweeping changes. A selection test (the 'eleven plus') was arranged in three parts. Most children were graded after taking Part I, but Parts II and III were given in cases where failure in the first part was very narrow.

According to the test results, every primary school child was directed at 11 into one of the secondary grades—grammar school, junior technical school, or the new 'secondary modern' school. There were no fees for the grammar school, and no child could enter it at 11 except on the result of the test. Some parents whose children did not reach the grammar school sent them to fee-paying private schools to avoid the modern school. It sometimes happened that bright children were transferred to the grammar school on a selection test at 13 (the 'thirteen plus'). When this was abandoned, an approved transfer might be made at 15. Where boys had left school at 15 to enter an apprenticeship, their employers were obliged to send them to the technical school for part-time continuation of their learning—the 'day-release' system.

In every case the Act laid down that education should suit the 'age, ability, and aptitude' of the pupil. On the vexed question of religion, schools were for the first time obliged to provide instruction. Parents could withdraw their children from the subject, and teachers could decline to give the instruction. A collective act of worship, as a school or in classes, was decreed to open the day, but the religious education could be given at any period of the school day.

There had never been an Education Act so advanced as that of 1944. It was supplemented and amended by further Acts in 1946, 1948, and 1952, but the basis remained the same. In spite of the hopeful expression 'parity of esteem', there was still a separatist outlook between grammar and secondary modern. However, a good modern school could produce teachers and university students.

Further developments provided generous grants for higher education, and where children had unsuitable clothing an individual grant of £8 to £10 was available. This was usually directed towards school uniform, which became of increasing importance

95

in the modern school. As the transfer at 11 meant transporting children from outlying districts in the 'catchment areas' of secondary schools, an elaborate system of bus season tickets, school buses, and even taxis was operated by the L.E.A. of each district. In schools not equipped with a canteen a meals service was arranged: each school with a canteen sent out meals in special containers carried by van or car to the outlying schools. These outgoing meals were cooked and placed in the containers about two hours before they were eaten, so the food was often apt to be soggy.

During the middle 1960s, the status of the technical college was further raised. There was no junior department then, and the age of entry was, in almost all cases, 16 years. This was allied with the promotion of the fifth-year course in modern schools (whose title was by then changed to county secondary schools). As the leaving age was due to be raised to 16 in the 1970s, the fifth-year course was useful in gearing up the schools for that time. There was a widespread movement towards comprehensive schools, broadly on the multilateral principle, and a great degree of coeducation (*41*).

41   Modern comprehensive school in Woolwich, 1956

EXPANSION IN EDUCATION

No survey of twentieth-century establishments would be complete without reference to the free discipline school. In this, the theory holds that education is infused by an informal atmosphere, with work done by choice at self-chosen times. Teachers and pupils are on the same plane of familiarity, so that Christian names are exchanged.

An outstanding centre of this kind was developed at Dartington Hall, in South Devon, under the headship of William Curry, a kindly, genial figure, who, it was said, was 'Bill' to the boys.

42   Teaching machine

Here the project method was of prime importance; the pupils made plans for a communal undertaking, like boat-building, and then carried out the project on their own initiative.

A. S. Neill's Summerhill was of even earlier date than Dartington, and Neill wrote numerous books on the advantages of progressive education. Though such schools maintained their places, it did not seem likely that the general school system would ever conform to their methods.

Other departures from accepted teaching methods include the teaching machine(42), devised by S. L. Pressey in the 1920s. It is designed to control the process of teaching; the machine presents information on a viewing panel, followed by questions on another panel, with a selection of answers. By pressing a button, the student chooses an answer, and the machine shows the result, with an explanation if the answer is wrong. All the work is arranged in progressive steps to constitute a complete study of the subject concerned.

In another mechanised process, programmed learning, a series of frames is prepared, building up knowledge of the subject in short stages. As with the machine, the sequence is: material; questions; answers; corrections. An eminent professor, when writing on these teaching aids in 1963, remarked that it was difficult to improve on the efficiency of the ordinary book as a transmitting device.

School design was developed by the 'open plan' (*43*), which dispensed with completely separated classrooms. Here was no fixed timetable, and no formal teaching as such, but simply advice by teachers. Though the scheme was widely supported by educationists, there were some practical problems not easy to solve. It presupposes that all the pupils, numbering hundreds, can be usefully and gainfully occupied in study on every school day. A particular problem is that a noise-producing practical class, e.g. metal-workers doing riveting, would make it difficult for nearby classes to concentrate on their own work.

43   Open plan school, 1968

Chapter VII
THE FARM

IN the early twentieth century Britain was importing at least three-quarters of the nation's food supply, so the farmer's vital work was directed towards making the most of home resources. In this he was aided by the development of the internal combustion engine. Though the earliest petrol tractors—first introduced in 1899—were clumsy and liable to break down when stones found their way into the exposed gears, they were the symbols of a new farming age.

Daniel Albone of Biggleswade designed the Ivel tractor in 1902, with a high chassis to keep the gears free of soil and stones. Around the rims of the broad back wheels were diagonal ridges to provide grip, with detachable angle-iron 'spuds' at intervals for the same purpose. This was the basis of the petrol tractors used on British farms early in the First World War.

In 1917, during the great farming drive, the Government contacted Henry Ford, who was responsible for introducing the mass-production system for the manufacture of cars. Ford applied his method to tractor-building, and in six months he had supplied 7,000 to Britain. His pioneer assembly-line for tractors was commemorated at the Ford factory in Basildon, Berkshire, in October 1967. A 1917 tractor made by Ford was on show, still in working order. These early tractors were suitable for ploughing and harrowing, and for use as power sources in threshing, but the tractor did not reach its peak value until the development of a light, all-purpose type.

A pioneer of the light tractor was the brilliant Harry Ferguson (1886–1960), whose design was in production by 1925. Such tractors were valuable for mowing and raking, and the various everyday farm tasks that call for mobility. It was forbidden to take the tractor on the road with the sharp-edged iron spuds on the wheels, as they damaged the road surface; the farmer had to fit broad iron rims over the spuds for road travel. This inconvenience was overcome early in the 1930s, when heavily ribbed pneumatic tyres were introduced.

44   Ransome tractor-plough, 1917

Mechanisation of this kind meant a change in the work of the farm labourer. Previously he had been thought of as a slow, dull son of the soil, but machinery improved his status. Nowadays the farm worker is no longer merely a labourer but a farmer-driver-mechanic, often with as much technical knowledge as his master.

There was one matter in which the farm labourer of the early twentieth century could make little progress. His wages had always been miserably low, even though he often had the advantages of a tied cottage, firewood, and dairy produce from the farm. An effort to regulate the widely varying pay scales was made in 1917, when an Agricultural Wages Board was set up, with a committee in each district. During its brief existence of one year, the Board fixed a minimum rate of 25 shillings a week—lower than any district wage at that time. After much discussion, the minimum for England and Wales was fixed at 30*s.* 6*d.* a week.

There was a steady increase in pay during the next three years, as prices for farm produce rose with the boom of 1920–1. At this period, a peak of 46*s.* 10*d.* a week was reached, but when the decline began, after 1921, wage cuts brought the figure down to 28 shillings. Finally, after the Agricultural Wages Act of 1924, a wage of 31*s*. 8*d*. was settled by 1926. It remained at that level for many years.

One unusual feature of wartime farm life was the formation of a force of women land-workers. This was designed to relieve the shortage of farm manpower caused by conscription, and the women gave excellent service. It was a reflection of the general wartime move in industry towards the employment of women in hitherto all-male work, and it had a grave effect upon the labour situation after the war.

45   Farm worker, 1914

Returning ex-servicemen found that employers often preferred to retain their trained—and cheaper—women workers.

Another influence on the post-1918 farm was the import position, for the dangers and difficulties of merchant ship traffic during the war had almost halved wheat imports. Whereas in 1914 Britain had taken her normal yearly quota of five million tons from overseas, the total fell to three million tons for each of the war years. This made home ploughing vital at the time, but the return of peace brought unrestricted wheat imports—up to six million tons a year by 1924. For that reason, the acreage under plough declined, and many British farmers turned their attention to livestock and dairy produce. There was a glut of arable-farming implements for sale by farmers who had given up trying to compete with the overseas producers. Where arable land was kept, it was used for feed crops, such as barley, oats, and greens.

In a country like Britain, with its irregular weather pattern, the farmer had formerly suffered losses through bad or unsuitable weather. A scheme to counter this was introduced in 1930 and developed in subsequent years, with varying degrees of success.

Basically, the scheme provided for Government direction of farm output sales. It was done by separate marketing boards for each product, as long as two-thirds of the producers of each commodity were agreeable to being directed. Each board decreed the conditions of sale.

Under the Wheat Act of 1932, farmers were paid a guaranteed standard price, made up as needed by payments from the millers. These payments, in proportion to the mills' output, were made to the Wheat Commission, who passed them on to the farmers. Another example of Government control was the milk scheme. Britain was arranged in 11 regions, each being controlled by an elected Regional Producers' Committee, and all committees were answerable to the Central Milk Marketing Board. Milk was sold at contract prices, either for domestic use or for manufacture. All receipts were then averaged by the Board, so that the producers were paid in proportion. There were penalties for selling at less than the fixed retail price, and a levy was paid to the Board by each producer according to the number of his cows. This was a great burden to the dairy-farmer.

One of the main features of this Government service was organised distribution, with fixed centres of disposal. At first the whole arrangement was viewed unfavourably by a considerable number of farmers; it was inconceivable that they should be regimented in such a way. Still, the thinkers among them appreciated that regulated distribution countered both glut and shortage. By their example in cooperation, and by discussions with their brother farmers, these pioneers greatly furthered the success of national marketing.

Though the farming community accepted official direction, there was one aspect that was a great burden from the beginning. Paperwork appeared on the farm—forms, returns, receipts, quantity checks, ink on fingers and table, and hair rumpled over tall columns of figures. Yet the development of Government controls proved extremely useful when the Second World War brought the farmer into the limelight again, after a long period of relative obscurity. Organisation and registration having been established for several years, it was much less difficult to take overall control of farm produce than it would otherwise have been.

At the outbreak of the Second World War, nearly a million people were working the land as farmers or employees. This total became nearly 1½ million before 1945 including the Women's Land Army, whose peak strength was 87,000 (1943). All the traditions of good sense, hard work, and cheerful willingness that had made the 1918 land girls famous reappeared in their successors of 1939. These girls were under the control of Lady Denham, their honorary director. All forms of farm labour were disposed of by County War Agricultural Emergency Committees, which also directed prisoners of war.

Produce of all kinds was strictly controlled; the making of cream was banned and the bulk of the farmer's milk output was collected in churns. Lorries collected these from wooden platforms built by the roadside near the farm, and returned the empty churns to the same place. At this time a large proportion of the nation's milk supply was converted into powder, which could be stored for long periods. It was reconstituted with water, though it was not much like the original when thus prepared.

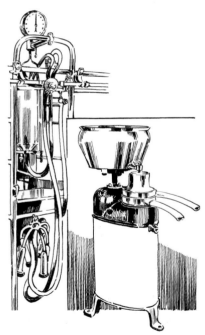

Because of the ban on cream a great number of farmers disposed of their cream-making apparatus, and for some time after the war cream was rather scarce. It had been two shillings a pound before production ceased, but when it reappeared it was 12s. 6d. a pound. Postwar scarcity and high prices were partly due to the lack of equipment, but the main reason was that the milk-collection scheme was preferred. Instead of processing the milk for cream and butter, the farmer simply placed his churns by the roadside for collection—a quick, trouble-free return. A large proportion of the milk went to centralised dairies for distribution, and the rest to processing factories.

Though supplies of cream

46 Type of Recording Milking Machine. Note glass container, scales, teat cups, and separator. *Courtesy of Alfa-Laval Co. Ltd*

were increased later, to form an important item in the dairyman's trade, the price never fell below nine shillings a pound. A type of commercialised cream was the chief output—separated or raw cream was scalded, which made it extremely thick and doughy. Traditional scalded cream is made by settling milk in pans over a gentle heat, which causes the cream to form a thick yellow crust on the surface. As this process involves heating all the milk, it is much slower and is not favoured.

In the separating method, milk is spun in a rapidly revolving bowl, without heat. Centrifugal force brings the watery content of the milk to the outer part of the bowl, while the lighter cream remains in the centre. Cream and separated milk are drawn off through different pipes, and only the cream goes for scalding.

On the wartime farm of 1939–45 all main foodstuffs were under strict Government surveillance. An egg-rationing scheme was brought into force at the beginning of the war. Each poultry owner with more than a certain number of hens was required to pass the majority of the eggs to a local grading station, where they were sized as large, medium, or small, and date-stamped. From these stations the eggs were sent to retailers. This was a complicated procedure with such perishable goods, and it was estimated that 17 million eggs went bad before the system was working smoothly. At best, more than two weeks elapsed between production and sale. In order to ensure that farmers surrendered the greater part of the egg output it was the rule that the number of eggs put into the scheme determined the amount of poultry feed that the farmer could buy. A great number of eggs were dehydrated and sold in packets as 'dried eggs'.

Many farm products were subsidised by the Government. Retail prices were fixed at a reasonable level for the buyer, but, in order to cover the farmer's increased costs, the Ministry of Food arranged for him to receive a higher figure than the retail price. For instance, a farmer might be paid four shillings a dozen for eggs taken to the grading station, but the same eggs would sell at three shillings in the shops. Subsidies were maintained after the war for various farm products, and the grading stations for eggs became a permanent service.

With the revival of arable farming, the plough once again assumed an important role. As in 1914, overseas supplies came in only at the price of blood, so an increase in home production was essential. Arable land was extended by breaking up large areas of hitherto unproductive rough pasture, and Government grants encouraged this.

In the original form of tractor-drawn plough, the two components had been separate—the plough resting on its own wheels, and linked to the motive unit. When the latter was dragging the plough, much depended upon a good grip with the back wheels of the tractor. Old-type spudded wheels provided this, but with the adoption of pneumatic tyres came a difficulty—there was less rear weight. Long before the problem arose in 1926 the famous firm of Ransome had produced a mounted plough (*44*), actually attached to the rear of the tractor. This plough could be raised or lowered by a spring lever, but because the weight problem had not then arisen there was no demand for the new device.

47   Present-day reversible mounted plough

During the late 1930s an American mounted plough came into use, providing rear weight, and the principle became general. It was a hydraulic system, containing oil under pressure, and through this advance the tractor-plough became much more handy in use. Thus, at the time when the British farmer most needed a manageable, mobile plough, it was at hand. However, in wartime the question of fuel was vital. Petrol was the life-blood of the armed forces, so a substitute fuel for agriculture was found in T.V.O.— tractor vaporising oil. It was a type of paraffin, operable in the sturdy tractor engines, though they had to be started with petrol.

These various aspects of the farm in wartime give us a picture of organisation developed by a degree of compulsion. A nation at war has to exploit her food-producing capacity to the utmost. For this reason, the Government's 'extraordinary powers' applied—a provision whereby the State could take any action deemed

48   Land Rover

necessary for the nation's welfare in wartime. If a farmer was considered to be working his land badly, he could be deprived of it. This actually happened in a few cases, and it gave rise to bitter comment by other farmers about ministry advisers without much knowledge of farming.

Wartime was a paper nightmare for the farmer. His returns of prewar days were nothing compared to the pile of clerical work required by declarations of output and applications for supplies. This was an addition to the endless tasks of the farmer's wife, who often lent her wits to the paper battle. It became a common practice to get professional help, particularly with the income tax tangle.

While American forces were in Britain, they made use of a small, sturdy type of open car that they called a 'jeep'. This was the name of a curious animal that featured in Popeye cartoons. Because of the cross-country abilities of this little vehicle, British manufacturers adapted the design for the Land Rover—part car, part van, part lorry(48). This and the 'shooting brake', with a van-shaped body, windows and removable seats, became the passenger-cum-light haulage units of the farm. In general, the expansion of the motor industry was of great value to the farmer in remote areas, making him and his family mobile as never before.

On a number of farms, petrol engines had been used for many years as power units, driving electricity generators. Output from these was limited, being chiefly employed for lighting. A Government move of vast importance was an Act of Parliament (1926) setting up the Central Electricity Board. This body was responsible for the National Electricity Grid, a network of overhead cables that stretched across country on tall girder-pylons. Their gaunt forms, festooned with heavy, drooping cables, aroused the wrath of nature-lovers, but the cost of laying the cables underground would have been enormous.

In 1935, when the grid was completed, thousands of rural dwellings, farmhouse and cottage, had the benefit of electricity for the first time. Gradually, the importance of the oil lamp, the candle, and coal and wood for cooking waned. A great turbo-drive generating station served each area, its output rising to 132,000 volts. This power was reduced through transformers to a low voltage, about 240, suitable for use in appliances. Though the supply was sometimes restricted at first, limiting the number of lights that could be used at one time, these teething troubles were in due course overcome, and full service was available by 1945.

On the farm, power was used to run milking machines (46), and dairies were fitted with sterilisers and hot water supplies. By 1950 the gradual spread of television had reached the farm, through the expansion of the power supply. In this way the last barrier was reduced. No country place was so remote that mechanical transport could not reach it. Radio had already brought in sound entertainment and with the advent of television country people could command a view of the outside world. This did much to erase the image of the cloddish yokel who knew of nothing but mangel-wurzels and draught horses. In fact, there had been an understandable decline in the latter. Where 668,000 farm horses had been in regular work in 1939, by 1950 the number was almost halved, and 10 years after that there were only 80,000 left in work.

Mechanisation brought its problems and tragedies. In ploughing a slope, the horse-ploughman could traverse it to and fro, to save his horses the recurrent climb. It was often dangerous to work across the slope with a tractor; a number of fatalities occurred

107

49   Post-hole digger, 1968

through overturning when this method was used, so tractors ploughed only downhill on a steep slope, and returned with the plough raised. Where it was necessary to plough across, a 'crawler' could be used. This was a low, tracked vehicle with a wide chassis which prevented it from capsizing at steep angles. The overturning of a tractor in the author's own district was saved from tragedy by the intelligence of the farmer's dog—that priceless piece of equipment which no mechanical aid can replace. When the tractor overturned, pinning the driver beneath, the dog raced back to the farmhouse, drew attention by its barking, and led the rescuers to the scene of the accident.

Sheepdogs have always been noted for their great sagacity. One instance, seen by the author, occurred when a large flock of sheep was being driven through a broad thoroughfare in Barnstaple, North Devon. Sheep filled the way from wall to wall, and the leaders showed signs of going up a small side turning. Behind the flock, the dog went once to each side, but could not squeeze past to get ahead. Instantly it jumped up and ran across the huddled backs to reach the turning in time.

It is difficult to see how the dog's services can be replaced, but in other respects farming is the target of constant experiment. Pest control, the countering of weather conditions, and high production at reasonable cost are the triple targets, with scientific aids as the weapon. Reading University is the Mecca of agricultural science, but there are a number of research stations up and down the country. Probably the questions of pest and weed control have gained most attention in recent years. The use of aircraft for delivering chemical sprays was pioneered in the 1930s (50), and 30 years later helicopters were being used for the work.

A number of writers have declared that crop-spraying is a two-

50 Spraying from an aeroplane against potato blight in Norfolk

edged sword, menacing humans as well as pests. In 1946 Friend
Sykes, a Salisbury Plain farmer, wrote in strong terms on mis-
treatment of the soil with chemicals. He supported the view that
the natural cycle of livestock grazing, and manure to feed the soil,
was preferable to the risk of human and livestock disease through
drastic measures. Air-sprays had the drawback of drifting, by
which means the poison was carried to crops that might convey
ill-effects.

During the winter of 1960–1 a group of farmers in adjoining
districts of Suffolk and Essex experimented with airborne sowing.
This treatment was intended for land that was too wet to bear the
weight of implements, and over 1,000 acres were sown by air under
rainy conditions. It appeared that air-sown wheat grew well in
fields of 50 to 60 acres, but in smaller fields the crop failed because
of excessive water. Further work was needed under two heads—to
make provision for covering air-sown seed, and to find a seed
dressing that would repel birds and would not be affected by
moisture.

While this work was going on to counter moisture, some

northern farmers were equipped for irrigation. Their apparatus consisted of about 1,000 feet of three-inch diameter pipe serving 24 sprinklers, and supplied by a pump at 500 gallons a minute. There was a distance of 24 to 30 feet between the sprinklers, which could deliver the equivalent of one inch of rain over 50 acres in 10 days, with pipe movement five times a day. An observer reported, after an official survey, that farms thus irrigated showed a 25 per cent increase in yields of potatoes and sugar beet, and 30 per cent in fruit.

Without doubt, the most prominent examples of increased production on the farm are in the egg, meat, and poultry sections. Under the traditional system of poultry-keeping the hens scratched around their runs to supplement their provided feed, and those to be killed were penned up to fatten. A twice-daily collection of eggs took place.

About 1918, the battery cage idea was introduced, whereby hens were kept in tiers of wire cages and given a balanced diet, so that they laid frequently(51). This system has been enormously expanded since 1945, and by 1967 at least 80 per cent of British hens were kept indoors on a diet of 'egg pellets'. It has been calculated that 28 million hens are in battery cages, and about the same number are in 'deep litter' with no cages but in partial darkness. In effect, the hens are egg machines, whose output is artificially stimulated to meet the national demand for eggs.

There is a certain amount of consumer resistance to mass-produced eggs; some people say that they are pale in the yolk and insufficiently nourishing. Others frankly deplore the means of rapid production, and boycott the battery eggs. For these reasons, there is a demand for free-range eggs, from hens that scratch about in the old way.

Egg production is only one expanded branch of the poultry industry; the other is the supply of 'broiler chickens'. These are reared under rigid control in large broiler units, with carefully graded feed, exercise, heat and light. After 10 weeks the birds weigh $3\frac{1}{2}$ lbs., and mass-killing plants are then operated. These deal with 4,500 birds an hour, killing, bleeding, and scalding them to make plucking easier. In spite of the plentiful flow of poultry into the market, and the consequent reduction of prices, some critics complain of puffed-up tasteless flesh on the mass-reared poultry, so free-range birds are in demand.

51   Poultry industry

There is much controversy about the rights and wrongs of the 'factory farm', which includes the trade in broiler calves. On British cattle farms about a million bull calves are born every year, but in this mainly milk-producing community most of those calves are unwanted. It was formerly the practice to kill these almost at once, chiefly for their fine skins, but now they are reared for three months in broiler units, to supply veal. As this must be white, the diet is arranged to induce a form of anaemia, and all sunlight is excluded. A high temperature is maintained in the unit, so that the thirsty calves drink great quantities of milk, and this, with lack of exercise, stimulates growth.

Under present-day conditions, the cattle-farmer has to keep pace with breeding developments, such as crosses to gain meat with little fat. He is aided by the vastly increased facilities for artificial insemination, so that the best bulls are made available to the everyday farmer. A further remarkable service is the extraction of an embryo from the parent animal to check the sex of the unborn

111

calf. If it is as required, the embryo can be returned to the womb.

When cattle were being transported in lorries, those with horns were liable to wound others when they were herded in together, so dehorning became a regular practice in the 1960s. An ultimate target is a hornless breed. Of course, disease is the bugbear of the cattle farmer, and here the whole might of science is on his side, with antibiotics and a battery of medicines. In mid-1957 a live vaccine for foot-and-mouth disease was being tested at the Diseases Research Institute, Pirbright, Surrey, but the results of their researches have not been made public. In the great foot-and-mouth epidemic of 1967-8, the only solution found was wholesale slaughter.

Farmers of today are exposed to much criticism for their methods of rearing sales stock, and their use of poisons on the land. It has been suggested that toxic substances in the soil kill friendly insects as well as pests, and that poison is conveyed to humans at second hand through crops from that soil, and through beasts that feed on its herbage. Another and more positive result has been the poisoning of birds and bees in serious numbers.

During the mid-1950s, British rabbits suffered an epidemic called 'myxomatosis', which destroyed countless thousands. At the time this seemed a good thing for the farmer, as it saved his crops from the depredations of the rabbits. However, the following lambing season was a nightmare. Foxes, which normally fed on rabbits, were short of food through the effects of the epidemic. As a result, they took hundreds of newly born lambs, so groups of farmers had to organise lamp-and-shotgun patrols at night. It was an instance of what happened when the balance of nature was disturbed, and naturalists read into it a warning. A fox-repellent powder is now spread around the lamb field.

On the up-to-date farm there is a great deal of Government direction, but it is balanced by the subsidy. For example, in a bad potato season the unsaleable crop was taken by the Ministry to avoid total loss to the farmer. As regards the farm worker, his pay is still low, with a basic figure of £11. 11s. (1967), but his hours are regulated. His day ends officially at 5 p.m., and extra work is paid at overtime rates. This is usually at harvest time, but that is not such a labour as in the past. In the cornfield, the combine harvester reaps, threshes, and stores the grain as it traverses the

52   Combine harvester

field. A straw baler can be attached, but that operation is frequently performed later.

When the first form of combine harvester appeared, on the great
2,000-acre wheatfields of Western America, it was composed of
separate machines. A steam traction engine drew the cutter, 42
feet wide, and behind that was the thresher. This assembly,
operated by eight men, could cut, thresh, clean, and bag 125
acres a day in 1890. While moving from one area to another, the
steam engine drew the water-wagon and cookhouse behind the
working implements.

Combine harvesters were used to some extent in England by
1950, in the self-contained form, though only large grain-fields
were suitable for its use(52). This implement is invaluable for
getting the crop under cover quickly. Present-day farmers often
cut their grain in the Western American style, by simply reaping
the heads and burning off the straw as it stands. Though this is a
convenient method, the National Farmers' Union issued a warning
at the end of the 1967 harvest that farmers burning off straw
should be careful to protect children, who might be attracted to the
blaze.

It is common practice for a farmer to hire a combine with driver, but many farmers still use the old self-binder whose sheaves are set up in stooks for carting away. If these become wet, a grain-drying plant is available in some areas, though the process is rather slow.

If one makes a general survey, British farm mechanisation compares favourably with any system in the world, and the standard of equipment is extremely high. British-made tractors, in particular, are tough and adaptable, with their wide gear range; the 12-gear Ford (10 forward, two reverse) has a clutchless gear change, because the gears are meshed all the time. A useful device for diesel tractors, which need mechanical starting, was the Simms spring-driven starting-motor; this dispensed with costly starting batteries.

Behind all these things are the hands and mind of the farm worker, whose livelihood is the land, and whose work makes the land live.

Chapter VIII
WORK AND INDUSTRY

FOR many centuries, coal and iron have been fundamental to Britain's economy. In coal-mining it was still manpower and the pick that won the coal in 1914. Grimy, perspiring miners, stripped to the waist, hacked at the coal face hundreds of feet below the surface, while patient ponies dragged away their never-ending loads.

British mining was done chiefly by the 'longwall' method, in which a section of the coal face, perhaps 100 yards in length, was cut back as a continuous operation. Another method, much used in America, was called 'bord and pillar'. Narrow galleries were cut at right angles to each other, so that the worked area consisted of many short coal faces, with square pillars at the intersections. In each case pit-props were set up and maintained to support the roof. These props were of conifer wood in 1914, and they would give warning of possible roof falls by groaning under the change of pressure. Many men consider that to be an advantage over present-day metal props, which give no such warning.

Miners have always worked under the triple threat of falling rock, floods, and gases from the coal-seam. Methane and carburetted hydrogen are among the gases present in coal, the latter forming 'fire-damp' (carbon dioxide). Gas and coal-dust form fire hazards as well, and the latter tends to affect men's lungs, bringing on a complaint called 'silicosis'.

It was not until some years after the First World War that there came any real move to make the miner's work less arduous and dangerous. A Government bill of 1911, the Coal Mines Act, had called upon owners to provide rescue facilities and first aid equipment, and in 1920 the Miners' Welfare Fund was established. This was financed by a levy on coal production. Its funds were used to provide help for the dependants of miners, and to build up amenities in the district. One important target was the setting up of pithead baths and changing rooms, so that the men could leave work in decent clothes instead of going home black. These baths were very few in number for many years.

Mines in Britain consist of circular shafts of up to 21 feet in diameter, sunk in pairs so that one provides a second means of access as well as ventilation. In general, the shafts are lined with masonry, concrete, or cast-iron, and they reach to a maximum of 3,000 feet in North Country mines. Main roads radiate from the bottom of the shaft, being about 12 feet wide and eight or 10 feet high.

By the late 1930s there was an increasing move towards mechanisation in the mine. For some years before that date the coal face had been broken up by the use of explosives. A worker called a 'shotfirer' made holes in the face with a pneumatic drill, packed in the blasting powder and tamped it down with stones. He exploded the charge with a battery.

A mass break-up technique like this led to the general use of the pneumatic drill instead of the miner's pick, so cables from a compressor led the motive power along the galleries to the coal face. Under the Coal Act of 1946 the mines were nationalised, and the pits were taken over by the National Coal Board. A total sum of £164¼ million was paid to the private mine-owners as compensation. There had been recurrent labour difficulties in the mines since the First World War, and during the 1939 War a great number of miners were called up for the Forces. When they were demobilised, many of them did not wish to return to the pits. However, this was partly offset by the development of coal-cutting machines (*53*).

In mechanical coal-working, the electric or compressed-air cutter is part of a unit for getting coal and transporting it to the shaft bottom for hoisting. Three band-saws form the chief components, two slicing horizontally along the coal face while the other makes a vertical cut on the same course. As the coal falls from the face, it is carried on a moving belt and deposited on the main conveyor belt, which takes it to the trams at the gathering point. When the trams are hoisted to the pithead, the coal is slid into a chute leading to the grading plant. Coal of less than three inches in diameter is passed through the coal washer before going on to rail wagons, while waste material is dumped in the vicinity.

Waste is a massive problem in mining areas, especially since new methods of disposal pulverise the material, making the great slagheaps liable to slip. In former days the base of a slag tip was formed of big masses, which gave a firm foundation. The appalling

116

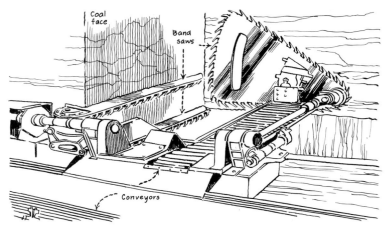

53   Coal-cutting machine

tragedy of Aberfan, in October 1966, was an example of the dangers of an ill-ordered slag tip.

Though mechanisation is the obvious means of coal-raising, it advances very slowly. Plans were made in the late 1950s for a fully mechanical pit, in which a cutter like that used for boring tunnels would be employed. From the working face, automatic gear would convey and load the coal, then hoist it to the surface. However, this scheme has not materialised, though most of Britain's coal is cut by machine. During the 1950s, the system of open-cast mining was further developed. This is appropriate where widespread coal deposits lie near the surface, and the soil is stripped in order to reach the coal. When the area has been worked out, the soil is replaced, and theoretically it can be worked again for crops, though farmers say that land so treated loses its usefulness.

One of the many coal by-products is the ironworker's coke. In the iron industry we can see a great change during the past half-century or so, especially in sources of supply. This will be more clear if we look back further still to 1875 when Britain was pro-ducing nearly half the world's supply of pig-iron, and $87\frac{1}{2}$ per cent of that was smelted from home iron ore. By 1914 imported foreign ore accounted for nearly 40 per cent while in 1955 the figure was roughly 70 per cent. Swedish ore was being brought in, for two good reasons—better quality, and lower working costs, as it smelted more easily than British ore.

For many years, in fact until the 1930s, it was usual to grade the quality of iron by fracture—that is, to break a piece and examine the edge at the break. Good-quality iron suitable for turning on a lathe shows a dark grey break with a large grain ('soft' iron), but 'hard' iron is white and close-grained. During the last 30 years grading by analysis has become the usual way of checking the composition of the metal. Under this system, 10 different grades are given, with many subdivisions.

Little change was to be seen in the actual casting of pig-iron from the seventeenth century until about 1930, except in the type of furnace. Even the name is a survival. A 'pig-bed' looked like a gridiron pattern of channels formed in a level floor of rammed moulding sand. It consisted of a number of main channels with secondaries leading off at right angles. Molten iron from the blast furnace flowed along the main channels until the whole pattern was filled. This was what caused some old-time foundry workers to say that the main channel looked like a sow with piglets. In fact, the bar of iron from that channel was still called the sow in 1950. While the pigs were still hot, they were separated to form sections of about a hundredweight.

A more up-to-date arrangement is the pig-casting machine, where an endless chain of permanent iron moulds is passed through a casting bay. Modern production methods demand a greater supply of pig-iron than the old system can provide, and the latter needs too much floor space.

Pig-iron is produced from a blast furnace that smelts ore to extract the iron. A furnace that produces molten iron for casting in moulds is called a 'remelt' furnace or 'cupola'. This was developed on the original blast furnace lines in the late eighteenth century, supposedly by the great iron-founder William Wilkinson, brother of the equally famous John. Remelting gave more opportunity to free iron from impurities, and the quality of the metal could be controlled. Both types of furnace had air blasts blown into them to increase the heat, but the smelting plant retained the name of the original.

During the middle years of the nineteenth century two forms of blast machine were devised, the fan and the pressure blower. In the latter, two sets of 20-inch blades rotating at about 300 r.p.m. built up a pressure inside the casing, so that there was a constant head of partly compressed air feeding into the wind-belt around the furnace. This blower and the multi-bladed fan, both driving off steam engines, continued in use until well into the twentieth century. By that time electricity was replacing steam power in foundry plant.

Most furnaces were blown with electric fan-blowers by the 1930s, but it is interesting to note that the great Carron Ironworks in Falkirk still used steam turbo-blowers in the mid-1950s. Each furnace had its own blower, which automatically adjusted itself to the resistance presented by the great column of coke, iron ore, and limestone in alternate layers inside the furnace. This attention to pressure was important. In the blast furnace of 1914 the great stream of blazing gases rose 20 feet above the funnel—in fact, seamen could use the light as a guide. Present-day blast furnaces have their tops enclosed, so that the hot gases are diverted through great pipes to do useful work in steam-producing, heating, and such services.

As blast furnaces run continuously, they are provided with some form of mechanical feed. One present-day system, based on an American suggestion of 1850, comprises an overhead track with a sheet-iron carrier running on bogies. Its bottom is formed by hinged doors, which drop the contents of the carrier into the 'charging bell'. This is the concave furnace top, which has a large cone suspended in the centre so that it seals the top to divert the gases as described. As the weight of material on the cone increases, it gives way, allowing the charge to fall through a central hole into the furnace, and a counterweight returns the cone to its place. Another method is the series of skips or containers on an endless belt, known as the 'skip hoist loader'. Each skip falls over at the top and shoots its contents into the furnace.

No elaborate charging gear was needed for the remelt furnace that served the foundry. Here were developed some of the ideas of the late nineteenth century. For instance, the continuous casting plant of 1930 was a much elaborated version of the 1890 system. A low-speed conveyor track carried an endless procession of moulds, which were poured as they passed through the casting bay. As the long, slow journey was made through the length of the foundry buildings, the small castings cooled enough to allow knocking out, while the sand from the destroyed moulds was conveyed to the reconditioning bay. There the sand was sifted to free it from pellets of scrap metal, moistened and cooled before being carried to the moulding machines. Automatic sand-slingers were in position, so that moulds were prepared without ramming, to keep the moving line supplied. In the foundry of 1914, everyone was black through contact with the blackened sand and coal dust, but the most up-to-date foundries are much cleaner. Mechanisation having been applied to mass production, the workers scarcely have to handle the sand at all.

All iron castings have a certain amount of burnt moulding sand sticking to the surface. Formerly this could only be removed with wire brushes, a dirty and tedious task, until two nineteenth-century ideas were developed to deal with extremes in size. One arrangement was the 'tumbling barrel' a revolving, horizontal metal drum, filled with small castings. In turning, these ground together so that they cleaned and polished each other. Large castings were dealt with in an enclosed chamber. Workers with protective clothing and masks used hosepipes to project high-pressure streams of sharp gravel against the big castings, which scoured and polished the surface. 'Sand-blasting' of this type was little used until after 1900, but by 1930 the system had been improved by the use of small-shot and was renamed shot-blasting.

In the present day, this is a way in which stone-deaf workers can be usefully employed. Their deafness means that the fearful din created in the shot-blasting has no ill-effect upon them.

Another branch of service by the blast furnace is the supply of molten iron for steel-making. In Sir Henry Bessemer's original process of 1855 iron was tapped from the furnace straight into a huge pivoted vessel, the 'converter', which was turned on its side to be charged with iron. Inside the bottom of the converter was a perforated plate, connected with an air pipe that was led in through one of the 'trunnions' or pivots on which the great vessel swung. As it was turned back to the upright, an air blast from the bottom plate kept the perforations clear, and forced a jet of air upwards through the metal itself. This air action caused all carbon to burn out of the metal, leaving pure cast-iron.

While the carbon was burning, a huge flame like a blowtorch was roaring from the converter mouth. It lasted about 20 minutes, then thick smoke followed. At that stage the metal was slightly recarbonised with a proportion of *Spiegeleisen*, containing 20 per cent of manganese; this created about 0·2 per cent of carbon to form steel, and dispersed gases that would have made the steel spongy. Bessemer steel is still made in the same manner today, though the quantity is much greater; in a large present-day steelworks a line of converters is drawn up to shoot their gigantic flames into the sky (*54*).

When the steel is converted, the vessel is pivoted to pour its contents—up to 60 tons—into a massive ladle on an overhead crane. This is a 'bottom-pouring' ladle—the metal is poured into a series of ingot moulds through a bottom trap in the ladle. Each ingot weighs between four and 10 tons, and the permanent moulds are made of iron. When an ingot is set firm enough to be moved, it is taken by an over-head grab to the 'soaking pit',

54   Bessemer converter blowing

where all the ingots are maintained at equal temperature for transfer to the rolling mills. There the ingots are squeezed between huge rollers, to form girders, bars, or sheets for the factory. In this process we see an elaboration of the early Bessemer plant, where the steel was poured from the converter into a ladle attached to a pivoted arm. A row of moulds was arranged in arc form within reach of the ladle. As present-day quantities are so much greater, the overhead crane is used to bring iron from blast furnace to converter, and steel from converter to mould.

Another steel-working system based on a late-nineteenth-century process is the open-hearth furnace. A trough of scrap steel is subjected to fierce gas flames from alternate directions. It takes about 14 hours of this treatment to melt 100 tons of steel, though the quality is better than in the Bessemer process, which could produce the same quantity in 35 minutes. Fine special steel is produced in electric furnaces, one type being based on work by Sir William Siemens and the French inventor Héroult. In the Héroult furnace, three electrodes create arcs which jump between fitments and steel, bringing the latter to a heat of well over 3,000°C.

121

55   Pressing out steel bodies in car industry

A high-frequency induction furnace was developed in 1922 by Dr Northrup, an American. By means of a high-frequency current passing through an insulated copper coil around the furnace, eddy currents are induced in the steel, with a stirring action which mixes alloys thoroughly. Northrup's furnace has the advantages of quick melting through high concentration of heat, with little loss.

Very little British steel is cast into moulds, so the rolling mills play a vital part. Much of the steel is drawn out into sheets for pressing in the massive machines which make possible the rapid production of the twentieth century. In pressing car wings, for instance, the great dies are shaped for the upper and lower faces of the wing, with cutting edges for trimming. When a steel sheet is placed upon the lower die the other is brought down with a squeeze effect that moulds the wing in one operation. An automatic motion presses the wing, raises the upper die, and checks it long enough for the wing to be exchanged for a fresh sheet.

All sheet-steel parts of a car are pressed in the same way. These great presses stand 20 feet high, and they weigh perhaps 80 tons, with a hydraulic pressure of 1,000 tons or more(*55*). It was the rise of the motor industry that brought the great advance in pressed steel work, but the initial cost of the dies alone often runs into several hundred thousand pounds for a complete set of car-body dies.

Since 1945, pressed steel has been used very widely in domestic equipment. Before the war, for example, gas cookers were usually made up of cast-iron parts, but present-day cookers are largely of pressed sheet steel. Some simple curves can be produced on a stretcher press, at little cost. A wooden 'former' supplies the curve, and a sheet of steel laid over it is gripped at either end, while the 'former' is slowly raised. Another type of press is used to work ingots that are too big to go under the steam hammer. These go for 'press forging', where the squeeze may equal 6,000 tons. Huge cranes with a lifting capacity of 300 tons do all the lifting and turning of the metal.

56   Machine-tool worker

All these are large-scale presses, but the advance in small, quick-repetition machines has been very rapid during the last 30 years. As with so many features of industry, the urgent needs of war speeded up production in a way that was invaluable to peace-time factories.

British steel-making received a great boost in 1966, when the invention of a new and vastly cheaper process in their laboratories at Sheffield was announced by the British Iron and Steel Research Association. It was successfully worked in the autumn of that year at a small pilot plant built by the Millom Haematite and Iron Company, on the coast of Cumberland. Iron flowing from the blast furnace was led off to the steel-making plant, where it went through a set of rings. There the metal was scattered under pressure, with lime blown among it, by jets of oxygen. Each tiny drop of metal burnt out 99·8 per cent of carbon, leaving the fraction necessary for steel. These drops were scattered upon a bed of hot steel scrap, with which they fused.

Steel-spraying was declared to be the most advanced steel-making technique in the world. It was done at a fraction of the usual cost, and the process was controlled from a push-button panel. A great advantage, too, was that the new plant could be added to existing blast furnaces, which brought the process near to continuous steel-making.

This kind of progress gave a new lift to the metal industry, but another great branch of British trade was suffering a decline at that time. For over 150 years, cotton had been an important and flourishing business, with a great variety of uses in clothes and goods. Until the middle of the twentieth century, an enormous flow of cotton came into the country, reaching a peak of a million 500-lb. bales a year by 1950. Manufacture and export on a large scale made cotton a great feature of the balance of trade, and nearly 1,000 million yards of cotton fabric per year were sold to nations all over the world (57).

There were three main reasons for the decline of cotton in the mid-twentieth century. Cheap-labour Eastern cotton goods had always been a threat to British cotton, and the threat was intensified when Japan was allowed to take part in the General Agreement on Trades and Tariffs some years before the Second World War. A second reason was the head-in-the-sand outlook of many mill-owners, who remained blind to the need for modernising their machinery. Even in 1955, old-style hand-loaded looms out-numbered the Northrop auto-matic self-loading shuttle looms by six to one. Those owners who postponed the purchase of new equipment could not afford to buy when the market began to fall. Last, but most powerful of all, was the de-velopment of superior man-made fibres.

57 Textile worker

Cotton manufacturers struggled gallantly against the intrusion of nylon and Terylene. Cotton materials attempted to imitate the qualities of these drip-dry, non-iron fabrics, but they were not equal in per-formance. Though cotton might be labelled drip-dry, synthetic fibres were much superior in that way, and cotton garments inscribed 'no-iron' still had to be ironed. In the unequal contest, cotton mill-owners fared much worse than the wool trade, be-cause there was no effort to mix cotton and synthetics. Among the wool traders, the danger was met by combining with new materials, so that 'Terylene and wool' became a familiar label.

By 1960 the cotton position had deteriorated so much that a number of Lancashire mills were converted to toy-making and light engineering. Though wool still holds a strong position today, synthetic materials of various types—from casein, seaweed, and other natural sources—have extended through the trade. There had never been a completely proof and non-condensing raincoat until rubberised plastic provided a fabric better than oilskin in those respects. This became so popular, as P.V.C., Cella, and so on, that young people adopted it for everyday wear.

In this age of technology, no invention had made a greater impact than the electronic computer (58). It is another example of the sword turned into a ploughshare, for the computer's origin lay in the anti-aircraft predictor of the 1940s. That device was of the type now called the 'analogue' computer, in which a variable quantity is represented by an electrical potential. As fed into the

58 Computer

predictor, the variables were the bearings and altitude of the target, and the time factor; these were combined with shell speed and the effect of conditions. This twofold problem of alignment was solved by the predictor.

Another type of computer is the 'digital' machine, in which the variable quantities are expressed by a two-digit or 'binary' code system. It has been compared with an adding machine in that numerical quantities are its basis. A great difference is the scope of work, for the digital computer has to store in a 'memory' a chain of operations for automatic action. With this, decisions are made by the machine to take a particular course of action according to the results of a previous operation, and all is done at a speed of perhaps a million operations a second.

Efficient work by a computer depends very much upon the skill of the operator in breaking down data into a suitable code for feeding in, and in ability to interpret the machine's findings. For instance, in the binary code which uses only 1 and 0, one hundred is represented by 1100100.

Since the computer was first produced it has passed through several stages of improvement. In the 1940 type, an electrical relay system was used, but this did not provide the speed of present-day machines, and the computer was more liable to error. About 1952 an improvement in both respects came with the use of vacuum tubes, with an alternative switching arrangement, and five or six years later a transistor machine was introduced. This permitted the apparatus to be cut down from a room-filling range of instruments to desk-model size.

Though the computer still has an aura of magic, it has become an everyday feature in many commercial centres. A remarkable example is its use in the spares section of a motor manufacturer's premises. Racks of spares are arranged in order, and covered by a computer-controlled selector arm. When a particular spare is passed out at the sales department, this is registered by the computer; the selector is guided to the appropriate rack, and a replacement is carried to the sales area. H. G. Wells' famous title, *The Shape of Things to Come*, may be truly applied to the computer's unlimited scope. On rare occasions one hears of a slip, as with the London lady who received a gas bill totalling thousands of pounds, but it would seem that computers are less prone to error than humans.

Our final example of machine-age development is in the factory preparation of food. This is a field of great twentieth-century advance. Though food-canning and preservation have been done commercially for 150 years in Britain, the peak of hygienic presentation has only been reached in post-1945 years. It is true that a famous chocolate firm pioneered this long before the war, but for general foodstuffs it was only the adoption of sealed plastic covers that raised the overall standard of hygiene in food for sale. With the vast increase in packaging brought about in that way, a similar upsurge in the production of wrapping machines took place (59).

It would be too much to hope that all packeted and preserved food is prepared in the way that a great chain-store concern shows, where all food items are specially selected for the firm, and cooking is done under clinical conditions. Most scrupulous cleanliness attends the packaging of food by a reputable firm; if the label reads 'washed sultanas', the housewife will find not a speck of grit on them. One of the favourite maxims of food-packaging

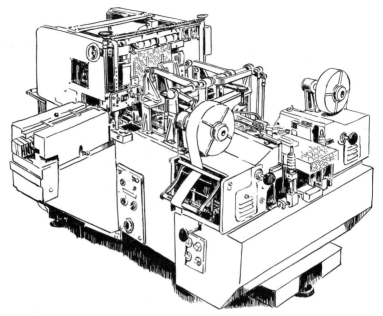

59   Wrapping machine, 1968

firms is 'untouched by hand'; it will be a great advance when all foodstuffs can come under this description.

One of the most impressive features of present-day industry is the existence of organised business 'cities', where the premises occupy many scores of acres. Here the worker is part of a great family, and his working conditions, his welfare, and his future are the active concern of the management and personal staff. This type of business, with its paternal care of apprentices, goes far to balance the industrial discontent that gains so much publicity.

Chapter IX
SCIENCE AND HEALING

THERE has been no more marvellous advance during the twentieth century than in the work of healing. One great early example was proving the origin of malaria, in which work British investigators played important parts. Sir Patrick Manson made a number of tests while working at Amoy, in South-East China, and in 1894 he established that certain insects were disease carriers. This was an important link with the findings of a French Army surgeon named Laveran, who reported in 1880 the presence of parasites in the blood of a malaria patient. Manson showed that embryos of the worm 'Filaria' were conveyed by mosquitoes and caused elephantiasis, a disease marked by enormous swelling.

Shortly after Manson's discovery his ideas were taken a stage further by Sir Ronald Ross (1857–1932), who identified the 'Anopheles' mosquito as the malaria carrier (1895–7). Ross(60) proved that a mosquito which had drawn blood from a malaria sufferer developed the parasites in its salivary gland, and planted them in the blood of the next person it attacked. During the next few years many experiments carried out for the London School of Tropical Medicine confirmed Ross's findings. In 1900 Dr Sambon and Dr Low went to live in a malarial district of Italy, and by covering themselves in a mosquito net at nightfall they escaped malaria entirely. Specimens of mosquitoes caught in the district were sent to the London School, where these insects transmitted malaria to people who had volunteered to act as guinea-pigs.

A positive action against the scourge was to treat ponds with petroleum, so destroying the mosquitoes at the breeding stage. This was not practicable on a large scale, so another defence was the draining of watery areas to dry up the breeding centres. For many years the only medicine for malaria patients was quinine. It was extracted from the bark of the Amazonian cinchona tree, and the sufferer was treated with 30 grains at a time. By the middle of the Second World War quinine was being replaced by less dangerous and more powerful substances, like plasmoquine and atebrin. In fact, these new remedies were a necessity; Japanese forces took over the cinchona plantations of Java and Sumatra, so that supplies of quinine ran short, and sickness mounted. After a spell of furious activity, American research chemists produced the synthetics that met the need.

After the Second World War, a large-scale movement against disease was instituted by the United Nations. It was entitled the World Health Organisation (1948), with its headquarters at Geneva, in the Palais des Nations. W.H.O. teams of worker-scientists attacked the mosquito scourge with D.D.T. sprays in the breeding areas.

60   Sir Ronald Ross

Malaria is not endemic in England, though we have mosquitoes, but the plague of influenza continues to make itself felt. This ancient disease was so named by sixteenth-century Italians, who believed that it was caused by the evil influence of a planet— hence *la influenza*. It is a most difficult sickness to combat, and it can be deadly where complications like pneumonia follow. Vaccination (*61*) is not wholly effective, for the virus tends to change into slightly different forms, requiring a new culture of germs to combat each form.

When the influenza virus is of a malignant type, the effect is disastrous. In 1918 a world-wide epidemic caused the death of 15 million people, which led the medical profession to take the disease more seriously than hitherto. In fact, a great number of doctors and nurses themselves caught the infection. Though science has not yet provided a shield against influenza, the often fatal onset of pneumonia can be countered with new preparations of the 'sulpha' group, and antibiotics.

The first scientist to contribute to the invention of these new treatments was Paul Ehrlich (1854–1915), a German Jew who found that certain chemicals and tissues had an affinity to each other.

This discovery in 1904 led to a long series of experiments with arsenic, which was at last rendered in a form called 'arsphenamine', commercially known as Salvarsan. Ehrlich's product was mainly for tropical diseases, but its significance lay in the fact that a drug had been man-made for a special purpose.

An important group of drugs known as 'sulphonamides' formed the next step in the anti-infection war. They were developed through the disclosure by Gerhard Domagk (1895–1964) that a dye known as 'Prontosil red' had valuable properties. It transpired, after Domagk's findings in 1932, that the active agent in the dye was sulphanilamide, a powerful antibacterial substance. French and

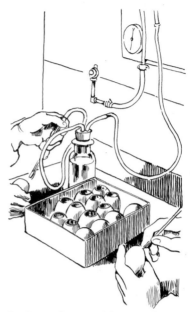

61 Preparing anti-flu vaccine in eggs at World Influenza Centre, London

English scientists expanded the original ideas by providing safer and more powerful forms.

When the sulpha drugs were injected, they did not kill germs, but disturbed their composition so that they could not divide and multiply. However, the dose had to be skilfully judged; if it was too strong, it might injure the 'leucocytes', the white blood cells that eat up invading bacteria. A weak dose simply allowed the germs to build up resistance, but a well-balanced treatment checked the germs' activity and made it easy for the leucocytes to devour them. Pneumonia germs could be checked in this way, and a few injections worked wonders. One of the most familiar of this group was the 'M and B' type of sulphonamide compound, made by the British firm of May and Baker.

These drugs were valuable in the war against disease, but in 1928 Alexander Fleming(62) found an even more effective weapon. He was one of the bacteriological team at St Mary's Hospital, in London, and his great contribution was made after preparing

62 Sir Alexander Fleming

some flat glass plates with layers of jelly on which to cultivate germs for observation. When one of the plates showed a patch of greenish mould, Fleming observed that the mould was killing the cultivated germs on contact. Further experiments proved beyond doubt that the mould, a common type named 'penicillium notatum', produced an organic acid that destroyed germs.

At the time of Fleming's discovery, it was impossible to produce 'penicillin' (so named from its origin) in large quantities, but this problem was tackled by a team of scientists at Oxford, led by Sir Howard Florey, in the late 1930s. Penicillin was proved to be the safest and most useful antibiotic, deadly to some types of germ, and harmless to the human body. Once the process of making penicillin had been standardised, large-scale production began in America. In the later stages of the Second World War an enormous saving of life was achieved among the wounded. Fleming was knighted in 1944, and a year later he shared with Sir Howard the Nobel Peace Prize. Ten years after this triumph Sir Alexander died, at the age of 74.

Another mould-extract chemical drug was produced in 1944—'streptomycin', composed of micro-organisms from earth mould, and valuable in the treatment of tuberculosis and plague. This powerful antibotic came from the laboratory of Dr Selman A. Waksman, but it had to be reinforced with other preparations, as the tuberculosis germ became resistant. In the constant search for weapons against those germs unaffected by penicillin, 'chloramphenicol' was found to be effective against typhus and typhoid fever (1947).

It was against typhoid that the first safeguarding experiment was carried out by the famous pathologist Professor Almroth Wright (1861–1947). He inoculated troops bound for the Boer War (1899–

1902) by injecting dead typhoid bacilli to build up resistance against the disease. However, the treatment was given only to volunteers, of whom there were few (three per cent of the total force), so the results were of little value. By 1913 the British Army authorities were convinced, and inoculation became a routine practice. Its effect was shown by comparative figures of infection and death rates. In South Africa 105 soldiers per 1,000 had been infected, and between 14 and 15 per 1,000 died, while in the 1914 war infection figures showed a little over two per 1,000, with deaths at 0·139 per 1,000. Another important form of inoculation of the 1914–18 period was for 'tetanus' (lockjaw), caused by a bacillus chiefly found in richly manured soil. This germ can only affect the human body through a wound, but when it does enter the body there are violent and painful spasms and paralysis. An efficient vaccine was introduced in the mid-1930s, and this was widely used as a protection during the Second World War.

Until the twentieth century brought relief, diphtheria was a scourge that carried off hundreds of English babies each year. It is an infectious disease, and germs may be taken in from a foul drain. A false membrane forms in the throat, and the patient may die by choking, or through general physical deterioration. Diphtheria germs might remain inactive in the throats of carriers, so the menace is only kept at bay by immunising. Before this treatment was arranged on a large scale for children in the early 1940s, there had been an average of more than 1,800 child deaths per year. Twenty years later the average was two deaths per year.

This was truly life-saving, and another such service concerned the once-fatal disease of diabetes. This disease affects the pancreas, a gland behind the stomach that contains chemicals for digesting fat, starch, and proteins. There are groups of cells in the pancreas that are called the 'islets of Langerhans', from which come the fluid that breaks up sugar. When this fluid is not produced, the body cannot reduce sugar properly, and the result is a decline of efficiency, coma, and death.

Until 1921, a diabetic's chances of survival were slight, but in that year a team of three men, led by (Sir) Frederick Banting (1891–1941) discovered the nature of the sugar-reducing fluid, 'insulin', and how to extract it from the pancreas of animals. By this means, regular doses of insulin and a carefully chosen diet could secure for the diabetic a normal, healthy life, where formerly death had threatened.

A further advance in healing was attained through a substance extracted from the cortex or rind of the adrenal gland, which aids digestion. As it was drawn from the cortex, the fluid was called 'cortisone', and it was effective for rheumatoid arthritis, some kidney and skin diseases, and asthma.

Just as diabetes had meant death in the early twentieth century, a sufferer from pernicious anaemia could not expect to live long. This complaint arises when the stomach fails to produce a substance that manufactures blood from food. Cases of secondary or minor anaemia (lack of red corpuscles in the blood) can be treated with iron salts, but nothing relieved the deadly type until two Americans, George H. Whipple and William P. Murphy, announced in 1926 a great success with a raw beef liver diet. The scourge was checked. More than 20 years later British and American scientists discovered, almost at the same time, the essential element in liver, which was named Vit. B12.

In addition to the great work on healing, twentieth-century scientists delved deeply into the question of nourishment. It was proved by F. G. Hopkins' experiments in 1912 that protein, fat, and carbohydrates were not enough—there had to be a balance of substances that were called 'vitamins'. This title was derived from a name applied to the group by the scientist Casimir Funk. He thought that these substances were 'amines', i.e. nitrogenous basics, but it was found later that their composition varied. Funk's term 'vitamines' was altered to vitamins by Jack Drummond, the English dietician.

It would be wearisome to give a long list of vitamins and two examples will be sufficient. Vitamin A, found in new milk, butter, egg-yolk, fish-oil, and spinach, is necessary for growth, and lack of Vitamin C, which is contained in acid fruits and greenstuff, causes scurvy.

While the science of medicine was building up its knowledge and skill, changes were also taking place in the world of surgery. Before the outbreak of war in 1914 a strict order of seniority was observed. Older, experienced surgeons tended to make the operating theatre a 'closed shop' by giving the idea to the young that only long years of service could fit them for the upper grades. The problem was increased by the progress of abdominal surgery

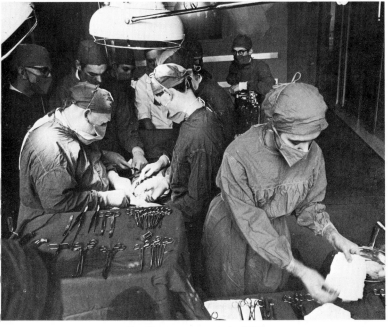

63   Surgeons at work, 1968

between 1900 and 1920. Probably the much-publicised operation
for appendicitis which Edward VII underwent when his coronation
was postponed in 1902 drew attention to surgery as a cure. It led
to similar operations at an earlier stage than before, so that the
death rate fell by 30 per cent, and deaths resulting from operations
became a rarity.

   In the hospital, some of the features that are now familiar were
only just creeping in in the early years of the twentieth century.
Rubber gloves were first worn in an American operating theatre
by Professor William Halsted before 1900, but by 1910 they were
common in English hospitals. Where formerly the surgeon had
operated in shirtsleeves or a bloody macintosh, the white gown
was in use early in the twentieth century. A white cap and a gauze
mask, first worn in 1920 at Charing Cross Hospital by Dr William
Hunter, completed the surgeon's equipment. At that date English
hospitals were using a mixture of ether and chloroform as an
anaesthetic.

With the outbreak of war in 1914 all regard for position and seniority among surgeons had to be sacrificed in the urgent cause of the wounded. Often it was the young surgeon, choosing for his patient a risky operation rather than certain death, who took the bold step that led to further life-saving. At a time when impossible demands on the surgeon were matched by unheard-of operations, a routine was devised under stress. Wounds had to be cleaned at the earliest possible moment; dead or mangled tissue was then pared away, and antiseptics such as hypochlorites were employed. These encouraged lymph to wash out the wounds.

During this nightmare period the system of blood transfusion was developed following the early work of the American doctor George Crile, who made a successful transfusion in 1906. This had been made possible by Landsteiner's classification of blood into groups (1901). Though transfusion was often invaluable where much blood had been lost, it was not always effective, for a strange reason. One of the perils of active service during the First World War was that of shock; a casualty might feel greater ill-effects from shock than from his wound. Apart from the general physical condition in shock, the blood became thickened and turgid, so that it moved slowly, and fresh blood was needed to supply the deficiency. However, not many surgeons were expert in this delicate work, so often a casualty with a slight wound died through the effects of shock.

Though a blood transfusion was the obvious thing, a thinner medium was needed where the patient's blood had thickened. During the war years experiments on blood itself revealed a thin, brownish fluid that was pure blood plasma. By 1918, shocked animals had been successfully treated with plasma transfusion, but human cases do not seem to have received this until 1934. At that time, the freezing and drying of plasma permitted it to be stored for up to five years, if necessary. In order to reconvert it to liquid plasma, it was mixed with sterile water. If whole blood was needed for transfusion in emergency, Type O was sought, as that could be used on almost anyone.

Before the great technical advances of the twentieth century, the surgeon was haunted by the clock. There were strict limits to the length of time during which the anaesthetic was effective, and there was no way of suspending or side-tracking the bodily functions. Increasingly bold experiment brought in such processes as feeding the patients through the veins (intravenous infusion) while the digestive tract was under operation. By means of continuous suction, any distension through gases was prevented, and the organs were rested and kept empty. This was achieved by 1926, and it was soon followed by a by-pass technique in which the patient's breathing was controlled by the anaesthetist during surgery on the upper chest. Until 1930 lung operations had always consisted of hurried, shallow cutting, but with the breathing assured, the surgeon's field of activity was greatly extended.

An even more notable advance was the improvement in heart surgery from 1939 onwards. Until that time an operation on or around the heart was hampered by the great flow of blood, so that the surgeon had to deal with this obstruction as well as the motion of the heart. These difficulties could be completely overcome by 1950, there being two methods of approach. Hypothermia or 'frozen sleep' was induced by putting the anaesthetised patient on ice or an ice-water mattress, so that the body temperature dropped by about 20°F. Less oxygen was needed to sustain life, and blood could be withheld from the brain for up to 15 minutes without damage, while the heart could be completely drained. A similar result could be gained with the heart-lung machine, invented by Dr D. G. Melrose of the Royal Post-graduate Medical School, Hammersmith Hospital, which kept up the circulation while by-passing the heart (64). In this way, if the heart was cooled it could be stopped for more than two hours, and restarted without damage.

All previous heart-surgery feats were eclipsed by the news that reached England early in December 1967. A 56-year-old South African had undergone an operation in which the heart of a young woman had been exchanged for his own. This

64 Heart-lung machine, 1962

extraordinary work was done by Professor Christian Barnard and a group of surgeons at the Groote Schuur Hospital, Cape Town. Eleven days later the patient was able to walk on the terrace, but he died a week afterwards. Another heart patient received a transplant a short time later, with apparent success.

Any such transplanting operation depends upon the body's acceptance of the new part. If the receiving tissues reject the transplant, it cannot knit in, and the operation fails. A number of kidney transplants were performed during the 1960s, with varying degrees of success, and the grafting of a new cornea to the eye is an accepted practice.

Team-work operations were a great feature of post-1945 surgery. In wartime England surgeons had been trained in specialist techniques—for head, chest, and face injuries, ophthalmics, and limb operations, with a particular class of neurosurgeons. It is a melancholy fact that war creates great advances in the art of healing, and in this case the system was maintained in postwar practice—the specialist, and the division of labour. Another great development from the same grim source was the use of alien materials for replacing faulty or damaged parts of the body. A pioneer in this was the American doctor, Charles Hufnaegel, who exchanged a defective heart valve for one of plastic in 1952. In present-day practice moulded plastics are freely used for joints and skull repairs, while plastic sponge is adapted for heart surgery. Large artery sections can be replaced with tubes made of Orlon, and in some cases inactive metals like vitalium and tantalium are introduced into the body as permanent repair material.

This application of foreign substances and mechanics gives the impression of a machine-minding team of experts in action, as in the use of the life-saving kidney machine. It is indeed an army mobilised with the weapons of present-day science in the face of disease and death. In the surgeon's hands the delicacy and precision of the razor-sharp scalpel; at the patient's bedside the anaesthetist with the needle for intravenous injection, and over the operating table the bottle of plasma at need. Surrounding all is the defence organisation against the enemy of infection.

Even the foregoing broad survey of medical science shows that both medicine and surgery command great resources. Though the action of some drugs is not fully predictable, an extraordinary range of treatment is at hand, so that a great percentage of elderly people have a daily pattern of pill-taking. It is ironical that, for all the advances in medical knowledge, the common cold still defies the doctor, though in Russia a mild form of radiation is employed to counteract it. In surgery an unceasing battle is waged against cancer, the scourge of present-day life. The cause of this disease has been the object of much discussion, and doctors disagree strongly on the question of whether or not there is a link between smoking and lung cancer. Possibly the increased use of radiation may take the place of cancer surgery, but until the causes can be identified, positive action will be restricted.

A third problem for medical science is the crippling disease known as infantile paralysis (poliomyelitis). This was alarmingly prevalent in England for some years after the war. Its effects varied from almost complete paralysis to a slight limp, and there was absolutely no certain evidence regarding either cause or transmission of the disease. At one time mosquitoes were suspect, as the incidence of polio appeared to be greater in hot weather, and several vaccines were produced, notably that of Dr Salk in America. However, without being able to isolate the germ all remedies were shots in the dark. There was no known reason for the scourge at the time, neither is it known why it is not so common today.

Chapter X
THE WELFARE STATE

CITIZENS in late-Victorian England were provided for if they were paupers (entirely without means) by two forms of charity. There was outside relief, by which food, clothes, fuel, and small sums of money were passed to the deserving poor at home. On the other hand, living quarters were provided for paupers in workhouses or 'unions'. All these arrangements were in the hands of local Boards of Guardians, and their respective systems showed every variation one can imagine. A few boards gave up dispensing outside relief after 1875, but at the other extreme were boards who continued to give most lavishly.

In the workhouse itself there was a fairly rigid classification of inmates, to avoid undesirable mixing of ages and types. Seven divisions were maintained, the first being those men who were infirm through age or illness. Able-bodied men were rated next, down to youths over 15, and the third class comprised boys aged from seven to 15. Women and girls were organised in three similar groups, and the last division consisted of children under seven. A separate ward was provided for each class, with subdivision where it seemed advisable (65). Married couples were separated as well, unless they were over 60. In that case, at the discretion of the guardians, the couple could be given a separate room. Those wanderers who came into the 'casual ward' for one night were kept completely isolated from the regular inmates, to avoid infecting them.

Where an entire family was in the union, the members would be in the appropriate wards, but they were allowed to meet every day. If they were in different unions, meetings were arranged at intervals. Under the Poor Law Act of 1889, the boards were directed to keep under their control boys up to the age of 16 and girls up to 18, as having been deserted by their parents, if the children were foundlings. A similar Act of 1899 extended the cover to orphans, and to children of cruel or neglectful parents. By the Custody of Children Act, 1891, if a child was abandoned, or was allowed to be

65   Victorian workhouse

brought up by someone else, the court had to be satisfied of the
parents' fitness to reclaim the child.

One form of institution for pauper children was the Cottage
Home, where the youthful inmates were brought up to be sent out
to work; the boys went to live-in on farms, and the girls to
domestic service. Special workhouse schools were provided, so
that segregation from other children was complete.

Poor Law provisions were made for the workless, too. The
London Boards of Guardians were given a number of special
privileges. Whitechapel Union could take in an able-bodied
unemployed man, and after 'a short detention', the man could go
out to seek work by day, while his family was given relief. Under
the old Outdoor Relief Regulation Order of 1852, the London
boards had leave to open labour yards for the workless, in which
stone-breaking was done to provide road-metal. In the Parish of
St Olave, a yard of that type was open between January and
March 1895, and 'relief' was paid at trade-union rates. This drew
such an enormous, unwieldy labour force that the yard was
swamped. Many of the men were of such low character that
genuine workmen did not care to join the company. There was so
little efficient supervision that a number of men only appeared on
pay-day.

It was very difficult to work out a scheme that would meet the

66   Down-and-outs, 1907—from a photograph

local government's circularised rules on unemployed workers. Relief should not imply pauper status by the nature of the work, and it must be of a type that all could do. No competition with those in regular work must be offered, and the work should not interfere with the resumption of regular employment. Local guardians were required to arrange matters, with two special conditions—the men employed should be recommended, and the pay should be less than they normally received. There is no record to show that any board succeeded in carrying out all these requirements.

In 1897, under Lord Salisbury's Conservative Government, the Workmen's Compensation Act introduced a cover for a limited number of skilled trades. This was to be provided by the employer out of his profits, and it concerned accidents that occurred during working hours. Though few classes of workers were included in the scheme (they were almost entirely engineers), it was the forerunner of Liberal welfare measures in the early twentieth century. An extension of the Act by the Liberal Sir Henry Campbell-Bannerman included a number of additional trades in the scheme, and two years later, in 1908, the budget of Herbert Asquith brought in the first British old age pension provision for retired workers.

Welfare schemes of the kind had been launched in France and Germany some years before, and the British plan was based on the German. It was non-contributory—no payments were required from workers—and the pension, which could be drawn at 70, was five shillings for a single man and 7s. 6d. for a couple. A watch was kept on the financial status of pensioners, and, if their means justified it, the payments could be reduced by one-shilling stages. Those people whose annual income was £31. 10s. or more did not qualify for assistance. An amendment raised that figure to £49. 17s. 6d., and the maximum pension became 10 shillings.

With this form of social security came two important moves for industrial workers. Advisory boards were set up under the Trade Boards Act of 1909, in order to fix minimum rates of pay in certain sweated industries—i.e. trades where pay was notoriously low, with long hours. Such trades as tailoring and lace-making were difficult to include in an ordinary union, as the workers were scattered, so these and other such trades were covered by the Act.

These trade boards comprised representative employers and workers, with some neutral members, usually as chairmen. Their rulings were legally enforced by the Ministry of Labour, under whose direction was made the other great effort for better industrial organisation. This was the setting up of 'labour exchanges' in 1909, to establish a pool of workers on which employers could draw. It was especially useful for those needing casual labour.

In those pre-1914 years was laid the foundation of the Welfare State. Lloyd George's National Insurance Act of 1911 was the next great step, and one that created very strong feelings on either side. Under this ambitious scheme, again based on a Continental precedent, a weekly contribution was made by the workman, the employer, and the State, paying fourpence, threepence, and twopence respectively. During illness, the worker drew 10 shillings a week for 26 weeks, and five shillings a week thereafter while he was still sick. (This did not apply to those over 70 years of age.) Medicine and medical attention were free, and sanatorium treatment was available. There was no provision for the worker's dependants, except that a maternity grant of 30 shillings was payable. Insurance under this act was compulsory for most workers earning less than £420 a year.

There was a great division of opinion on the Act. Its supporters quoted Lloyd George's phrase 'ninepence for fourpence', and stressed that friendly societies and trade unions, with their great experience in such matters, were being used in administration. In the opposite camp, employers and many workers objected to the stamp-card. There were numerous cases where stamps had not been affixed, though the worker's contributions had been taken by the employer. A national service of this kind, with its 'panel' of patients, was disagreeable to a number of doctors, who felt that it lowered the dignity of the profession.

Though these arrangements were relatively small in scope, they did form a barrier against utter destitution through sickness or unemployment. For the latter, the second part of the 1911 Act provided a similar three-way system, so that benefits could be drawn by the workless as a right, not as charity. About $2\frac{1}{2}$ million workers were covered by the Act, which did not include farm workers or those in subsidiary industries. Other features of that socially minded era were widely diverse: they included the first payment of a salary to Members of Parliament, who received £400 a year in consequence of the Parliament Act of 1911. In 1912 the Shop Hours Act directed that shopworkers must have a half-day holiday per week.

During the First World War, with its atmosphere of tension, there was no chance of further social development, except the admission to the franchise of women over 30. Mines, railways, and some hospitals were nationalised—the effect of this was to appear later. Victory was followed by bitterness and unrest. Factory workers, brought down from unheard-of wages to normal levels, were incensed. Many returning soldiers found no work, and post-war prices outstripped wages. This was a severe setback to the Welfare State idea, especially as Britain's vital overseas trade was crippled: many of her Continental customers were themselves in a state of bankruptcy. When British employers began to cut down on staff, the burden fell upon the relatively young unemployment insurance scheme.

By 1922 there were two million workers drawing the 'dole', and the Government was forced to divert other funds to the department. This difficult period culminated in the General Strike of 1926. One of the sources of discontent was the return of the mines to private ownership after the war. Miners suffered most over the strike; they remained out of work for four months, and the shocking misery of the Welsh mining valleys was a blot on Britain for many years.

It seemed, during the interwar years, that all hope of advancing the social security plan was vain, for mass unemployment became a permanent part of the social system (67). Some effort was made to put the workless on large-scale public operations like land reclamation, but the great capital outlay required discouraged the idea.

Among the workless apathy was easily developed, and many came to rely on the dole and outside charity. One parent known to the author at that time refused to let his unemployed son draw the dole, saying that if the young man joined the queue at the Exchange he would not *want* to work after a time. In spite of occasional fluctuations, the number of workless remained too high—in 1930 the figure was roughly 2½ million. By that time the dole was heavily subsidised, so financial juggling

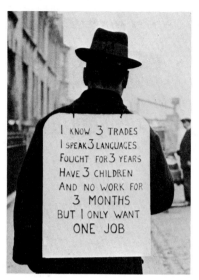

67 Man seeking work (interwar period)

had to be done—insurance contributions were raised, and the dole was cut. A Government plan that raised great outcry was the Means Test for the unemployed, which was described by newspapers as the 'Mean Test'. Officials visited the houses concerned and ordered the sale of non-essential belongings, so that the money thus gained could be used to support the family. Only when this money was spent could the worker draw the dole again.

Under the economy drive the salaries of public servants were reduced, including those of teachers, police, and civil service workers, and these lower levels were maintained until 1934.

There was no advance in social security until after the Second World War, though unemployment was eased by rearmament in the late 1930s. It was in 1941 that the first movements of a great postwar upsurge began, however. This activity took the form of a widespread social survey organised by Sir William Beveridge, a prominent Liberal politician. He was appointed Chairman of the Committee on Social Insurance and Allied Services, and the Beveridge Report was published in 1942. Most of its suggestions for an improved system of social security were accepted by the

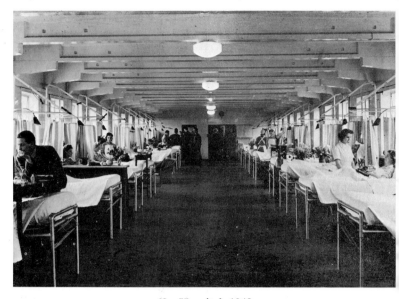

68   Hospital, 1948

Churchill Government, and filed for postwar implementation. A National Health Service on a non-contributory basis was listed among the Beveridge priorities, with more benefits, and a minister to coordinate the work. All classes of people were included— 'duke and dustman will contribute'.

When the Labour Government took office in 1945, its declared policy was to provide universal public benefit, so that every citizen was protected from the consequences of sickness or unemployment. By arranging that everyone should pay for the scheme the Government hoped to convey the idea of benefits drawn as a right. An early action, in June 1945, was the grant of family allowance. On each child of the family, apart from the first, a weekly payment of five shillings was made by the Government (raised to eight shillings in 1964).

Under the National Health Act of 1946, Aneurin Bevan, Minister of Health, brought into action a system based on the Beveridge Report, by which the 1911 Act was greatly expanded. All administration was done through Government channels, and friendly societies did not play an important part in distribution, as they had before.

146

In fact, the provisions of the 1946 Act did not come into force until 1948. When the plan was operating, it provided an all-embracing system under direct Government control. Some hospitals had been nationalised during the war, but all were brought in at this stage, to be controlled by Regional Hospital Management Committees. Every insured person, with the family, would be listed for treatment by a particular doctor, who was paid originally 15 shillings a year for every patient on his list. That sum was much increased later. At first spectacles, false teeth, and surgical appliances were free, but before long there was a return to the former system of proportionate payment.

In the same way, prescriptions were free, but such abuses occurred that a charge was imposed later. People would obtain a prescription for items that they could well buy themselves, such as

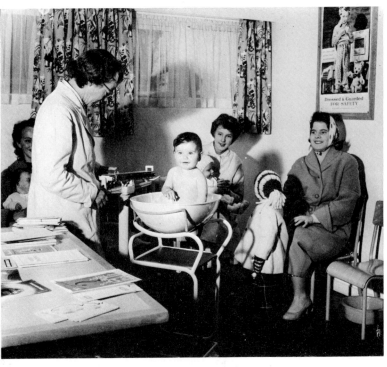

69   Children's clinic

cotton-wool. It has been said that in the first year of the new order the estimated cost of the service, £140 million, was exceeded by £68 million. However, when a charge was required, the situation steadied. For a time the charge remained static at one shilling per prescription, but in 1963 it was raised to two shillings per item on the prescription—a serious hardship for old people and low-wage workers. Under the Labour Government of 1964, prescriptions were again free, until economic crisis led to a charge of 2s. 6d. per item being imposed in 1968.

It was part of the overall arrangement that health centres should be set up under county councils, and the doctors themselves were responsible to local executive councils.

There was a three-way support in financing the National Health Service—the Exchequer, the local rates, and National Insurance contributions. Included in the latter were all the provisions of the social security plan under the National Insurance Act of 1946. This referred to the Ministry of National Insurance, established in 1944, and the Act was brought into force, with the National Health Act, in July 1948. Compulsory insurance of all males between 16 and 65 and of all female workers between 16 and 60 was required by law.

Unlike the 1911 Act, the only contributors were employer and worker. In 1948 the rate was 4s. 7d. a week for men over 18, and 3s. 7d. for women, with variations for self-employed and non-employed people. Workers' wives who were not employed could pay 3s. 8d. a week to receive a pension independent of their husbands. (In 1967 this scheme was abolished, and wives who had paid until then were informed that there would be no benefit.) If the wives were at work but did not wish to pay the full rate, they paid fourpence a week 'industrial insurance' to cover accidents while working.

In cases of sickness or unemployment, the worker received benefit at 26 shillings a week, with 16 shillings for his wife, and 7s. 6d. for a child. For a single person the retirement pension was 26 shillings as well, while a couple received 42 shillings. Women workers on maternity leave were paid 36 shillings a week for 13 weeks, with a £4 grant, and widows over 40 drew 26 shillings a week—33s. 6d. if she had a family. Men over 65 and women over 60 who chose to go on working had two shillings a week added to their pensions for each extra year of work. Other benefits included

70   Employment exchange, 1949

death grants, at rates of £20 for those over 18 down to £6 for a child under three.

A third Act of immense importance was the National Assistance Act of 1948. This brought the final destruction of the old Poor Law, which had been concerned with local relief funds; the Government now took up the matter direct. National Assistance Boards were set up throughout the country, to consider cases in the light of the applicant's income; capital or material possessions did not count.

This service expanded enormously during the succeeding 20 years. Old people with nothing but their pensions could draw a 'supplementary pension'—actually it was regular National Assistance more gracefully named. Those pensioners living in council quarters could have rent and rates paid, with occasional free issues of coal. A number of old people's homes and rent-free flats were available as well(*71*). An old lady wrote to a women's magazine in the winter of 1967 on this subject. She had been a domestic servant, and had always longed to live in a big house, with servants waiting on her, and to enjoy every comfort. Her ambition was realised, she wrote—life in a State-run old people's

71   Old people's home

home provided her with the big house, the servants, and everything she needed, including new clothes.

Those workers on short time whose income did not come up to a certain level could apply for a supplementary income—£4. 6s. for a single householder and £7. 1s. for a couple. If the applicant needed money urgently, he could ask the local office of the Ministry of Social Security for an immediate money grant of £8. This extra help had been provided for unemployed people as well, by the Ministry of Social Security Act (1966) and the National Insurance Act of that year. An assessment was made of the applicant's previous occupation and earnings, to find his customary level of living. On this was based the amount of extra unemployment benefit.

Ordinary unemployment or sickness benefit in 1967 rated £4. 10s. a week for a man, with £2. 16s. allowance for his wife. There was £1. 5s. for the first child, 17 shillings each for the second and third children, and 12 shillings each for any others. Those children who continued in full-time education to the age of 18 were reckoned in the family allowance grant. This was eight shillings a week for the second and third children, with 10 shillings for others. In cases where people took an orphaned child into their home, a guardian's allowance of £2. 2s. 6d. a week was paid.

One of the outstanding features of the Welfare State was the provision of legal facilities for the lower-income groups. Legal aid and advice, under an Act of that name passed in 1949, were given free in deserving cases, though the person seeking help was examined on his income. This service made available a solicitor to represent a poor man who otherwise could not possibly have afforded it.

Disabled people were very well provided for in a number of ways. A disablement pension scale rated a 100 per cent case, such as the loss of a hand or a foot, at £6. 15s. a week. This could be supplemented by a further £4 a week, with dependants' allowance, if the applicant was incapable of earning more than £2 a week. Invalid motor-carriages were available where the disabled person needed special transport to distant employment.

There were other aspects of social security too numerous to recount here. For instance, during industrial disputes, the strikers could have their hire-purchase commitments kept going from National Assistance. As the scheme took no account of capital, a house-owner might sell his property for several thousand pounds, and yet draw upon the public funds for income.

Our survey of social security shows very small beginnings, but throughout half a century immense strides have been made in providing for those in need. By a ruling of 1966, a man with three children and less than £20 a week could get half his rates paid for him, and the Government urged the public to take up such benefits. Free school dinners were available for the three children if the father's net income was not more than £13 a week, with free milk, orange juice, and other concessions. If an adolescent reached the age of 18 without a trade, Government training centres were available to teach him one. There was no upper age limit, so workers in any declining trade, or those in danger of dismissal as redundant, could apply for training in another trade.

Of course, there are loopholes and abuses in connection with the service, while the funds required are obtained by very heavy taxation, and high insurance contributions. A man's weekly payment at the end of 1967 was 15s. 8d. In some cases wartime measures have been retained, such as the continued levy of purchase tax, which, in luxury goods, returns to the Government half the sale price. If visitors from overseas fall ill, or have an accident while in Britain, they are allowed to use the National Health Service. This is a great concession, for in most Continental countries visitors have to pay their medical bills themselves. However, those who come to Britain with the set intention of obtaining treatment are expected to pay.

Chapter XI
ENTERTAINMENT

IN spite of the intrusive 'living pictures' of the cinematograph, the theatre and music hall enjoyed undiminished popularity in 1914. Inquisitive people patronised the cinema, but the darkened hall and the element of risk restrained the public. Only a few years before, on 8 January 1908, fire panic at a cinematograph exhibition in Barnsley had cost the lives of 16 children, trampled down in the rush.

Apart from other considerations, the cinema was too new for faces to be familiar, while the music hall in particular was full of old friends. It was not high-level entertainment—frequently there was vulgarity—but the music hall enfolded its patrons in a friendly embrace. On the stage were the dazzling illusionist Lafayette and the conjuror Chung Ling Soo—from Lancashire, but what of that? Harry Lauder was there, with knobby, twisted stick and rolling Scots accent, delivering with tremendous gusto his own compositions, such as 'I love a lassie', and 'Stop yer ticklin', Jock!'

Outstanding among the women who shone before the footlights were Vesta Tilley (born Matilda Alice Powles, later Lady de Frece), the first great male impersonator, and Marie Lloyd(*72*). The latter was held in most affectionate regard by the public. A Hoxton girl, she had been baptised as Matilda Alice Victoria Lloyd. She was typical of the profession in that her open-handed generosity was a byword. At frequent intervals she would descend on Hoxton to provide the street-urchins with clothes and shoes. Scores of pensioners were supported by her charity, and it was reckoned by a famous dramatic critic that Marie Lloyd had earned and given away £200,000.

At one time the ultra-popular entertainer was appearing at the Oxford, the London Pavilion, and the Tivoli in succession every evening for months. Admirers would go from one of these one-show-per-night halls to the next, to enjoy her performance several times over. During the First World War her rollicking 'I'm one of the ruins that Oliver Cromwell knocked abaht a bit' played a great part in keeping up morale. This signature tune, as a later audience

72   Marie Lloyd

would have called it, was on her lips when she collapsed on stage at the Edmonton Empire in October 1922. Her death, at 52, was like a national calamity, bringing tears to the eyes of the Cockney world.

While the music hall drew its nightly audiences with traditional shows, the legitimate stage was undergoing a revolution. Its audiences were being educated into a new type of play, in the style of Henrik Johan Ibsen (1828–1906), the Norwegian poet and dramatist. Ibsen's satires and realistic drama had aroused fierce opposition early in his career, but by the 1890s he was acknowledged to be the greatest living playwright. One of the most prominent of Ibsen's disciples was the controversial playwright George Bernard Shaw (1856–1948), whose prolific output delighted (or scandalised) both contemporaries and posterity. J. M. Barrie and John Galsworthy were other notable members of the Ibsen school.

Shaw's 'Three Plays for Puritans', 1901, were written for his friend, the beautiful and talented actress Ellen Terry (1848–1928), who had formerly played Shakespeare as Sir Henry Irving's leading lady. Sir Henry, who managed the Lyceum Theatre from 1878 to his death at 68 in 1906, was the first actor ever to be knighted (1895). At the Lyceum his superb productions made the theatre famous. Another distinguished knight of the stage was Sir Herbert Beerbohm Tree (1853–1917), who managed the Haymarket and His Majesty's in turn. He himself was a Shakespearian actor, though he often appeared in other plays.

At the opera, the dashing Gilbert and Sullivan works still drew a mighty following. Gilbert's death in 1911 had made no difference to the immense success of those lively operas, which surpassed all before them in their witty and sparkling lyrics. It is easy to see why theatrical performances held their own in the face of growing cinematograph competition. However, this was increasing. An obscure music-hall turn, the 'Eight Lancashire Lads', included a little Cockney boy, born in Walworth. This young performer, Charles Spencer Chaplin, later joined the comedians who did acrobatics in Fred Karno's 'The Mumming Birds'.

In 1910 Chaplin went to America, where he made a number of short comedy films for the Keystone Company. At that time

73   Charlie Chaplin in 'The Kid'

David Wark Griffith (1875–1948) was just making his debut with his first film. Griffith was an actor with a keen military bent, which expressed itself in the captions for the films he made. He was a strange mixture of sentiment and ruthlessness in his approach to film-making technique; everything was subordinated to the idea of making the audience *see*. In Griffith's hands the film was a construction with innumerable parts, each to be watched and guided into place, so that the audience was given a complete survey of each aspect of the play.

Griffith's first great film, 'The Birth of a Nation' (1915) with a Civil War setting, was a good example of his handling. In producing it, he had the whole concept in his mind, without script; the scenes were shot on his direction, and he edited the results. This producer had a magnificent touch; he could conceive great spectacles, sweeping panorama, enormous crowds. In making his second great film, 'Intolerance' (1916), he once arranged a camera in a captive balloon, which was brought down slowly into the midst of the set.

As Griffith made meticulous plans for each film, the great Russian producer Sergei Eisenstein (1898–1948) was his counterpart in precision. In his internationally famous 'Battleship Potemkin' (1925) there was high drama, superb setting and direction, and a tragic message. This postwar period showed a

155

wide diversity of styles. German film-makers specialised in the macabre, like 'The Cabinet of Dr Caligari' (1919), the story of a mesmerist's direction of a sleep-walking murderer. Historical and propaganda films were made by the Russians, and in America the film star was publicised.

Britain's infant film industry was cut down by the First World War, and there was no revival until 1920. Even then, America's enormous wealth, and the long start given by the war, kept her far ahead of Britain. Limited studio space and facilities meant that, whereas Britain was making 60 films a year by 1950, America was making 400. Development in the industry was marked by great mergers producing companies such as J. Arthur Rank and Warner Brothers.

Amid the horrifying and dramatic in early films, the ex-Keystone character Chaplin made history as the pathetic comedian. During the war years when Britain's film-making was at a standstill the Englishman in baggy trousers, bowler hat, and turned-up boots swaggered his cane through the American studios. Chaplin has been called 'the first genius among screen actors'. He became a much-loved international figure, able to produce fits of laughter or convey heartrending pathos in turn. With Jackie Coogan in 'The Kid' (1921) he captivated the film-going world (73).

A completely different appeal was exercised by the swashbuckling film hero Douglas Fairbanks, born Ullman (1883–1939).

74   Rudolf Valentino

He was the ideal dashing adventurer, with spectacular gymnastic feats, irresistible swordsmanship, and devil-may-care manner. Fairbanks was at his best in such films as 'The Three Musketeers' and 'The Thief of Baghdad'. His wife, Mary Pickford, was 'the world's sweetheart' for her winsome film parts at the end of the First World War. In the middle 1920s came the brilliant, brief career of the handsome Italian, Rudolf Valentino (1895–1926) who was the first great screen lover (74).

156

He excelled in desert stories like 'The Sheikh' and 'Blood and Sand'. Valentino's early death in 1926 evoked an extraordinary public reaction. Hundreds of women in both Europe and America went into deep mourning, and more than one spiritualist believer swore that she was in touch with the screen idol.

Already a greater star was rising, for Greta Lovisa Gustafsson, known as Greta Garbo (75), entered films in 1922. She had trained at a dramatic school attached to the Royal Theatre in Stockholm, her birthplace. Garbo was considered by millions of filmgoers to be the film actress of the century. Her beauty, her superb presence, and her unforgettable art made her completely unique. Among her many outstanding successes were 'Mata Hari', 'Queen Christina', and a delightful light-hearted 'Ninotchka'. With a wisdom extremely rare in a top-ranking star, Garbo left the screen at the height of her fame, to live in retirement.

For many years after their inception, films were shown with dialogue in sub-titles projected upon the screen. This developed the cinema pest who read the passages aloud, and often a child would insistently demand the reading. In 1927 'talking' films were first made public by Warner Brothers. These 'talkies' were synchronised with a taped dialogue, including effects, and some quaint situations arose when the earliest short support films were put on. Occasionally the synchronised sound would go out of alignment, so that a character might be seen walking to a telephone while talking into it. Conversely, he might be holding the telephone with his mouth working soundlessly.

The first feature talking film that was shown in London,' The Jazz Singer', starred Al Jolson. He was a Washington actor whose real name was Asa Yoelson; his second important film, 'The Singing Fool', was one of the greatest box-office successes of the time.

Sound films did away with

75   Greta Garbo

157

'effects' behind the screen, and provided their own music, so cinema musicians became redundant. In the developed sound film, a perforated sound track ran along the edge of the film. Its punctures were 'read' in passing through the projector, the sound being sent out by amplifiers behind the screen. This gave the cinema a great boost in its constant battle with the legitimate theatre, for live sound had been the latter's main advantage. During the late 1920s began a series of 'Follies' films like 'The Broadway Melody', which were immensely popular in Britain.

At that time, film-making had gained another success by introducing colour cinematography. This was first seen in the pioneer Smith and Urban 'Kinemacolor' of 1906, and the later efforts were still rather crude. One of the first big Hollywood musical films shown in England was 'Rio Rita' (1929) with Dolores del Rio and John Boles. This was a typical early colour effort, with somewhat lurid effects and heavily fringed-in colour masses.

A popular feature at the time was community singing by the audience, the words being projected on the screen with a little ball of light moving along in time with the music. These song-films were called 'Cartunes', a reference to the comic-strip type of coloured film that was made popular by Walter Elias Disney of Chicago (Walt Disney). His famous character Mickey Mouse, who first appeared in the 1928 film 'Plane Crazy', became a household word. Disney followed it with other creations like Donald Duck, Pinocchio, and so on. An enormous number of coloured drawings were made and photographed for each film; the first of Disney's full length film-cartoons was 'Snow White and the Seven Dwarfs' (1938). It took three years to produce, and consisted of 477,000 photographed drawings, with delightful colour effects.

During this period, in the larger cinemas, there was the added attraction of performances on the huge Wurlitzer piped organ, which rose from the basement to the level of the auditorium while being played. Another feature, which was not repeated, was the early attempt at a stereoscopic system by issuing the audience with viewing frames. These gave the picture the effect of added depth.

In general, the introduction of sound and colour films were the two major advances in the industry. During the later 1950s, 'cinerama' effects on a wide, curved screen gave the audience a greater impression of reality. Otherwise it was only the degree of magnificence that made a film outstanding in a technical sense.

Cecil Blount de Mille was famous for his immense, lavish productions, such as 'The Sign of the Cross' and 'Cleopatra'. From about 1955 onwards there was a progressive decline in cinema-going. Whereas in 1948 it was calculated that 28 million visits a week were paid to cinemas, 20 years later the figure was down to below three million. This was due to the development of broadcast entertainment.

Long before, during the early days of Guglielmo Marconi's wireless telegraphy, Professor John Fleming of London University had invented the radio valve in 1904. For the next 15 years radio was largely confined to morse code signals. However, in 1920 the great singer Dame Nellie Melba broadcast from the Marconi Works at Chelmsford, and by 1922 a number of radio manufacturers had formed a limited company. They broadcast under licence from the Postmaster-General, and this was the origin of the London transmitting station, with the call sign 2LO.

Sound broadcasting was achieved by converting the speech or music at the source into electrical impulses, each representing the sound that set it up. Output from the studio was regulated and amplified in the control room, from which a land line took the impulses to the transmitter. A powerful carrier wave current, generated by the broadcasting station, took out and dispersed the impulses from the transmitting station to the tall broadcasting aerials.

As the radiating waves of impulses were diffused they were received by aerials linked to self-contained radio sets. When these sets picked up the waves, they amplified and strengthened the tiny currents that the waves set up. Next, the currents were separated from the impulses of the original programme, and the latter were passed to the loudspeaker, which reconverted them to the original sounds and amplified them.

There were some difficulties with early receiving sets—interference was often very bad, and sometimes lightning struck the tall domestic aerials. In 1924 the author, as a schoolboy, lined up with his colleagues to 'listen-in' with a pair of headphones to a set (with 40-foot aerial mast) brought to the school by a kindly local resident. A few seconds of crackle and buzz, interspersed with snatches of music from a brass band, constituted the treat. Headphones were the original listening system, a legacy of the Morse Code days, but the loudspeaker was in use by 1923. It looked like a distorted

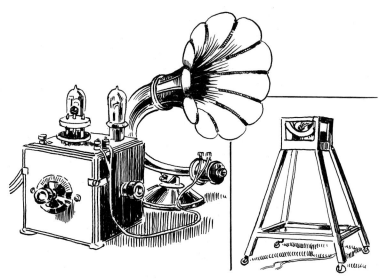

76   Radio set and microphone, 1924–5

gramophone horn, from which it obviously derived(76). In addition to valve receiving sets there were short-range sets of the cat's-whisker type, with sensitive antennae instead of valves.

A registered office at Savoy Hill was the centre of the British Broadcasting Company, with two studios in the building. By 1924 the system was in full swing, with Rex Palmer as 'Uncle Rex' in 'Children's Hour'. There were some curious features, such as the arrangements for broadcasting dance music, with a microphone suspended from the ceiling. Dancers passing below the microphone occasionally called out a greeting to someone whom they thought might be 'listening in', as it was called then. An engineer was on the alert to cut out these unwanted intrusions.

In the studio of 1925 the microphone was a Round-Sykes Magnetophone, embodying a heavy magnet and a very light mouthpiece set in sponge rubber on a wooden frame. This assembly was supported on spread-out legs on castors. For the sake of sparing timid artistes, the grotesque shape was hidden in a rectangular cover draped with blue silk. Studio operatives called the structure the 'meat safe'. As the microphone was sensitive to excessive vibration, a singer with a powerful voice had to be stationed perhaps 40 feet away from the stand.

ENTERTAINMENT

At the outset 2LO broadcasts had a limited range, but in July 1925 the Company set up a new high-powered transmitter at Daventry. From that station news of national importance could be received practically all over the country. Daventry sent out its own programmes, being linked by land lines to Savoy Hill, and this led to a great increase in the London output from several new studios.

Less than a year after the increase in broadcast coverage the General Strike paralysed the country and closed down newspaper offices, so that only a single broadsheet was on issue, the *British Gazette*. A similar one-sheet paper was brought out by the strikers, the *Workers' Gazette*. This scarcity of news could have caused grave public uneasiness in a crisis but the British Broadcasting Company's new powerful transmitter carried news bulletins at frequent intervals. These were made available to the public by shopkeepers and other private owners of receiving sets, who placed loudspeakers where the public could listen. One of David Low's cartoons of that time showed a crowd listening at a shop door.

Over a million people held receiving-set licences, so early in 1927 the Company was granted a Royal Charter as the British Broadcasting Corporation. Control was vested in a group of governors, under the supervision of a Director-General; Sir John (later Lord) Reith was the first to hold this office. The organisation was made responsible to Parliament, though it was not actively controlled as regards output or policy. One of the most successful aspects of broadcasting was launched in the same year—the B.B.C. broadcasts to schools. These were first arranged by Sir Walford Davies (1869–1941), the famous organist and composer.

By that time, wireless affairs were of great public interest and enthusiasts discussed 'wave-lengths'. These are variations in the strength of electrical waves sent out by transmitter aerials. When the charges of electricity from the transmitting station surge up and down the aerials, every completed movement is called a 'cycle'. Each cycle sends out a wave which travels at the speed of light (186,000 miles per second), and the number of cycles per second is graded as the 'frequency'. Those waves that travel over the ground lose energy, so short waves are used for long-distance international broadcasting. High-level sky waves can go for very long distances, rebounding from the ionosphere (the upper-atmosphere levels).

Medium and long waves are used for short ranges, thus maintaining their strength.

An international agreement on broadcast wave-lengths had been reached by 1925, though Germany and Italy used these for propaganda. English foreign-language broadcasts were made regularly, and by 1938 a network of programmes was going out to America and Europe. By that time the B.B.C. had left Savoy Hill for Broadcasting House, Portland Place (May 1932), soon after the setting up of the Empire News bulletin in January. At the end of the year Empire News was replaced by Empire Service.

In 1940, regional broadcasts were severely reduced, but the 'Forces' programmes of that year provided light entertainment for troops and workers. At the end of the war the Home Service and the Light Programme were established (1945), and in 1946 the intellectual Third Programme began. These titles were changed in October 1967, when the British stations were numbered—the Home became Radio 4, the Light was broadcast on two stations, Radio 1 (pop music) and Radio 2, while the Third was renamed Radio 3.

Programmes on the radio fell into four main categories: drama, including some splendid Shakespearian productions and serialised classics; music, in classical, light, and popular styles, much of it on records; variety, with the famous Vic Oliver as compere of one particular show for many years; and instructional broadcasts on a wide range of subjects. In the post-1945 era, the 'disc jockey' was a feature of record programmes; one of the earliest well-known disc jockeys had been Christopher Stone, whose dreamy and apologetic style could be heard during the 1930s.

These entertainments made a good deal of difference to home life and social affairs. When a favourite programme was being broadcast, callers and conversations were not welcomed. As time went on, though, and radio became familiar, it sometimes provided an unheeded background for conversation. One practical use for music broadcasts was the factory system of 'music while you work'. This idea was introduced during the Second World War to lighten the dullness of work in munitions factories. In mechanical, repetitive jobs lively music helped production, providing the volume was not excessive.

When radio aerials had been fined down to permit a self-contained set in the 1930s, portable receivers became popular. These were powered by electricity from the mains, batteries, or both. A great advantage over the fixed set was that the portable could be turned around if interference was spoiling the reception.

At that time, car radio sets were being fitted in increasing numbers. They had been tried out by the Daimler Company in 1922, but interference from the engine had caused the firm to abandon the idea. Ten years later these difficulties had been overcome, and the motorist could enjoy his entertainment on the road, by means of an interior aerial, or the telescopic mast on the wing. This sort of thing was much advanced in the years following the Second World War, when small radio sets were fitted to bicycles with long, flexible aerials. During the 1960s the valveless transistor radio has become immensely popular, some being of pocket size. It is a common spectacle to see young people with transistors in hand or slung over the shoulder, listening to a programme as they walk. An up-to-the-minute hat design for men of 1967 had a small transistor built into the crown.

While radio broadcasting was still in its infancy, the marvel of television was being developed. The first step towards its invention was taken in 1873, when the nature of the non-metallic element called 'selenium' was realised. Its electrical properties varied according to the degree of light upon it, showing that light could be converted to electrical impulses and conveyed by a current. Over 30 years later a scientist named Campbell-Swinton showed that light impulses could best be transmitted and received by 'cathode-ray' tubes (1908). There matters appeared to rest until just after the First World War, when the first stage of television transmission was successfully reached.

The man responsible for this was John Logie Baird (1888–1946), a Scotsman from Helensburgh. He had abandoned a business career to work at the fascinating quest for radio vision, and on 27 January 1920 he actually demonstrated this in London. Baird's apparatus was on show at the great Wembley Exhibition of 1924 (77), and on 10 February 1928 he brought off an experiment that made his name ring around the world. From a transmitting room in the City, he conveyed pictures of a Mrs Howe and several other people across the Atlantic, to be picked up at Hartsdale, on the outskirts of New York. This historic range of pictures was seen on a tiny 2 × 3 inch square of ground glass, and the viewers numbered four—two directors of the new Baird Company,

77 John Logie Baird with original television low-definition transmitter, 1924. (*Inset*) Television set of 1935. First transmission of the human face. Low definition (30 lines)

the owner of the Hartsdale site, and a man from the Reuter news agency.

In order to line up the Americans' sets for reception, a ventriloquist's dummy was arranged before the television camera. When all was clear, a telephoned request for people to be shown came in from New York. Several people complied, moving their heads in turn before the camera, and the historic transmission was carried out. Baird used a medium wave-length, which the ionosphere could reflect back to earth again, and a system known as a mechanical scanner.

This was the first transmission of actual pictures, though the American inventor Jenkins had sent crude silhouettes across the ocean about six months before. Baird's pictures were extremely coarse in texture, with low definition in 30 lines, which were clearly visible. By 1935 it was possible to obtain 180-line pictures, and the standard 20 years later was 405 lines, a much clearer and sharper picture. Just as in a piece of fabric, if the thread is coarse and thick, it is visible and not many threads are needed to make up the width of the piece. In fine material the threads are so thin and numerous that individually they are almost invisible. It is exactly like this with the lines making up a television picture.

By 1934 the cathode-ray system had been further developed, and the B.B.C. began the first public television service in the world on 2 November 1936 at Alexandra Palace, in North London. As our picture shows, television screens of those days were no larger than a cigar box. Viewing was a considerable eyestrain, in a room that was completely dark. A radius of 35 miles from London was served, though the range could extend another 10 miles under favourable conditions.

No further development was made until 10 years later, owing to international crises and the outbreak of war. In June 1946, the broadcasting of television was resumed with the Emitron camera, a cathode-ray instrument devised by the Marconi-E.M.I. Company for use by the B.B.C.

In its simplest form, the cathode-ray tube was a glass bulb, with a small amount of gas in it. At each end a metal electrode was sealed into the glass, the two being 'anode' and 'cathode' respectively. These terms are based on Greek words—*anodos* (way up) or positive, and *cathodos* (descent), implying negative. A high electrical potential difference passed between the two electrodes as cathode rays, driving a discharge current (electrons) through the gas.

This arrangement is varied in the application to television. One end of the tube is painted with fluorescent material, which lights up on receiving impulses. While the cathode is left in place the anode is moved nearer to it, so the cathode rays pass through a small hole in the anode, to strike the fluorescent screen at the end.

At the receiving end, the picture is presented on the flattened end of the cathode-ray tube, through the magnifying of the tiny light impulses that came in. On the tube end, which represents the screen, the fluorescent material cools the inner surface. This material has projected against it a stream of electrons through the 'gun' or hole in the anode at the neck of the tube. By this means a varied pattern of light and shade is produced, according to the number and force of the electrons. This pattern is a reproduction of the scene transmitted. Pictures are built up at the rate of about 25 a second, and, in order to make the stream of electrons scan the screen, magnetic deflector plates are set around the tube.

78   Modern television set

In the studio, under batteries of Kleig lights, the Emitron camera is mounted on a trolley, with overhead microphones near by. A separate, windowed cubicle above the floor level houses the producers, while sound and vision are each linked to an amplifier. Both output stages are checked on a monitor in the cubicle, and the output then passes to a central control panel. Transmitters convey the impulses to the vision and sound aerials on the broadcasting mast, from which they are radiated. As the first H-shaped aerials begin to sprout over the rooftops, it was the dawn of a new entertainment age.

With the postwar upsurge of television, the B.B.C. asked the public for ideas on a shortened name. One or two ideas, e.g. Video, were much favoured by the Corporation, but viewers voted heavily in favour of simple TV., which was adopted.

Makers of television sets vied with each other over the larger screen, so that the small nine-inch type was soon superseded. Screens of well over 20 inches became common by 1958, and reception was improved by adjustable brightness (78). Interference was a great hazard in the first postwar decade; the passing car or the neighbour's power drill produced electrical disturbances that made the screen look like a firework display. However, shielding devices and the use of suppressors did much to abate the nuisance.

As a home entertainment, television rapidly took over first place. A news broadcast became more immediate when people could actually see the scene in question, and the movements of the figures. Films could be viewed in the comfort of home, and variety shows were also available. One of the advantages was the glimpse of far-away places which many viewers would not otherwise have seen. Though much of the entertainment was of a popular kind— quiz competitions, e.g. 'Double your Money', and the long-lasting

166

'Coronation Street'—some remarkable cultural programmes were also broadcast.

Just as with radio in earlier days, a group of personalities became familiar in every household—Peter Scott, enthusiast on wild life; Vera Lynn, beautiful and melodious; Sir Mortimer Wheeler, military archaeologist; the irrepressible Harry Secombe.

During the year 1955–6 the first commercial programmes were shown under the Independent Television Authority (I.T.A.), Associated Rediffusion Limited; the first show was broadcast on 22 September 1955. This organisation ran a huge variety of entertainment and more serious programmes, interspersed with advertising matter in the American style. It was under I.T.V. that the first cash prize quiz was established. A number of new commercial television contractors started business in the same year— the A.B.C. Television Company, Granada Television, and others.

An interesting result of television coverage of show-jumping and athletics was increased attendance at the actual events, as if a

79   The Beatles on television

glimpse had whetted the appetite. For outside broadcasts, each centre had its own equipment, with a mobile control room and three Image Orthicon cameras. A number of 'roving eye' vans carrying cameras were provided for on-the-spot interviews. A special technique was required for such interviews, but they were immensely popular with viewers.

For some time after the beginning of public-service television, it was not possible to establish a regular transatlantic broadcast service. Baird's broadcasts on the medium wave-length were made at chosen times, when the ionosphere was high enough above the earth to reflect his signals. As the ionosphere varies in altitude according to the season, and even by night and day, it could not be used for regular transmitting. In any case, large-scale broadcasting used up too much of the impulse-band width to make use of the medium wave practicable. For this reason, television broadcasting was confined to ultra-short waves on a non-reflecting course. However, in 1961 the Americans launched their Telstar communications satellite which could maintain a constant altitude to reflect signals, and so solved the problem.

Only a few months after Baird's transatlantic triumph he was able to demonstrate a system of colour television (July 1928). This was not developed at the time, nor did it gain significant notice until the Americans reported successful experiments with colour in 1953. Tests were then begun at Alexandra Palace in 1955, until, in August 1966, it was announced that a colour service would be available for two-thirds of Britain's viewers by 1967. At the time, the B.B.C. was making tests on the West German system, and the lowest price for a 25-inch colour set was £250. On Saturday 2 December 1967, the first British colour service was begun on B.B.C. 2.

Chapter XII
ROAD AND RAIL

FOR some years after the English motoring laws were relaxed in 1896, motoring was chiefly a pursuit of the wealthy. In 1904 the great Rolls-Royce organisation began building cars, under the partners Charles Stewart Rolls (1877–1910) and Sir Frederick Henry Royce (1863–1933). Sir Henry founded the engineering firm of Royce Ltd, in 1884, and he designed the engine for Rolls' car, which the latter drove in the Monte Carlo–London race of 1906.

It is a pleasant thought that the magnificent Rolls-Royce engine is still the best in a highly competitive trade(86). These stately cars were of large size, and the 'Silver Ghost' of 1906 created a great stir at the Olympic Motor Show of that year. Subsequently the Rolls bodywork was built exclusively by Henry Jervis Mulliner, one of the 120 motor pioneers who founded the Automobile Club of Great Britain and Ireland in 1897. Mulliner himself designed a 'Silver Ghost' body in 1908. This type of Rolls was fitted with the Silent Knight sleeve-valve invented by Charles Knight of Wisconsin, U.S.A. His device provided cast-iron sleeves or liners inside the cylinders. By this means, Knight claimed, noise was greatly reduced.

When Edward, Prince of Wales (later Edward VII) became a car enthusiast, his patronage of the 1897 motorists' group gave it an added status, and 10 years later it was renamed the Royal Automobile Club. Just before that, in 1905, the other great motorists' organisation had been formed by those who sought protection against police-traps set up to catch speeding motorists. This led to the establishment of road patrol scouts by the Automobile Association and the R.A.C.

In those prewar days, a tiny seed was planted in a district of Oxford known as Cowley St John, from which a mighty commercial empire was to grow. In 1893 William Richard Morris(80), a Worcester-born lad of 15, began an apprenticeship in bicycle manufacture. By doing this, he stifled his great wish to be a surgeon.

After only nine months, William left his employer because of

80　Lord Nuffield

the latter's reluctance to increase the pay, and the boy set up in his father's James Street house to build and repair bicycles. His first machine, made with factory-supplied parts, is still preserved at Cowley. This youthful mechanic rode his own products at cycle-race meetings, and gained the championships of three counties in distances up to 50 miles. Through these successes, business boomed, and Morris opened a shop.

An obvious step for a bicycle enthusiast was to venture into motor-cycle work, and in 1901 Morris built a low-powered machine with success. After that his activities with motor-cycles were successful in practice, but not completely profitable. Though he made a good deal of money, he had entered into partnership with unfortunate results, for the money was misused and lost. Having then set up alone a cycle and motor-cycle repair shop at Longwall, Morris ran a garage for a time. At length he worked out the idea of a small car, low in price and running cost, to bring motoring within reach of the man in the street.

At first Morris' plans were rather vague, until the Earl of Macclesfield became interested and decided to back the young mechanic. Practically all the parts for the 'Morris Oxford' of 1912 were brought from various firms. However, Morris' garage experience with different cars had made him a shrewd judge of quality. His own car was not actually ready until the spring of 1913, but so many well-known manufacturers had supplied parts that the car was sure of attention. It was produced in quantity at Temple Cowley, an old military training college (*81*).

When the Oxford was running it tended to steam at the radiator. Morris declared that this was due to unsuitable plugs and wanted to use Bosch plugs, but some patriots objected to the use of a German product.

Accounts by owners of some early Oxfords—these have been called 'Bullnoses', owing to the D-front radiator—give a good insight into motoring during the war years 1914–18. Bullnoses were almost certain to skid if foot or hand brakes were put on hard—both had to be used together, lightly. They would do 55 m.p.h. easily, but at this speed road-holding was poor, and the plugs overheated. Radiator water was blown out by steam forming around the exhaust valves, so that a canvas bucket had to be carried to refill the radiator. On the other hand, motorists praised the easy steering, clutch, lack of brake-fade and general reliability of the Oxford.

Early in 1915 the 'Morris Cowley' was advertised, with an American engine, at 158 guineas. It had electric lights as standard —previous Morris cars had acetylene, with oil rear lamps—and a dipstick oil check. This model was tested over rough, trackless country without ill-effect, and it was widely commended. In addition to private cars, a number of Morris omnibuses, vans, and lorries were to be seen on the road.

A Government order of 1915 stopped the importing of motor parts except for commercial building, so the Morris car line was reduced. When the war was over, restrictions prevented him from renewing the American contracts, so the firm was unable to profit by the postwar boom period. After a long search, Morris found the French firm of Hotchkiss, who were able to supply engines.

81   Morris Oxford, 1913

82   Examples of Ford Model T. Tower 1914 (*left*) and Sedan 1923 (*right*)

Production at Cowley recommenced in September 1919, though it was slow to build up.

A thorn in the flesh of all British car-makers was the booming sale of Ford cars in England, both before and after the war. Henry Ford (1863–1947), born in Michigan, had been designing cars since 1893, and he had produced Models A, B, C, F, K, R, and S before he brought out his famous Model T in 1908.

Ford is noted as being the first factory owner to bring in mass production and the assembly-line method, though the former was not in fact a new idea. It was the cheap car that was the designer's real contribution to the trade—so cheap that no British maker could compete.

This was shown in 1921, when the sales boom in England faded, and Morris was left with a huge stock of cars on his hands. Matters were made worse by the fact that the American boom had receded still earlier and Ford had reduced his prices in both America and England. With remarkable courage Morris slashed his own prices, by £100 in some cases, and the move was immensely worth while. However, he was still much above his rival's prices; a 1921 Morris Cowley four-seater, at rock-bottom cut price, was £341, while the five-seater Model T Ford was only £195.

Though the Model T(*82*) was extremely tough and reliable, with good spares and after-sales service, it looked the same as it had in 1908, and it possessed some drawbacks. It backfired at the start, with peril to wrists; unless one rear wheel was first jacked up, in cold weather the drag of oil in the gearbox would make the car creep up on the motorist who swung the starting-handle. Brakes, steering, and equipment were far from good, but the car would go anywhere; in fact, Western American farmers used to run it tyreless along the railtracks. Ford was most shrewd in his provision for service; he had factory-trained mechanics scattered through America in his company's second year.

With an increasing number of small cars on the road traffic provisions were needed, and the familiar white line was first employed in the early 1920s. It does not seem possible to establish an exact date for this innovation: the A.A. records show that, during the period named, the Association defrayed the cost of painting experimental white lines on some Brighton roads. An older institution was the practice of driving on the left. This was never law; the idea arose from a recommendation issued at Lancashire Quarter Sessions on 6 August 1795. Several accidents having occured through ill-regulated traffic, owners of carriages were advised 'to give directions to their servants, and to all coachmen, postilions, waggons, carters, etc., to observe the following rule in driving, viz., always keep on the left side of the street or road . . . by keeping on the left side of the street or road is meant that every driver shall keep his left hand to the wall or fence.' In 1967 Sweden changed over to driving on the right, leaving Britain as the only Western nation to maintain left-side driving.

In the *Autocar Handbook* of 1920 there is a flyleaf announcement regarding 'the largely increased number of new owners on the road'. In view of this, the publishers proposed to issue separate books on driving and on the small car. Road traffic of that period was classified in the *Handbook* as heavy steam vehicles, including traction engines: heavy petrol transport, such as omnibuses, lorries, vans, fire engines, etc.: 'autocars' for passengers: motor-cycles and 'cycle-cars', three- or four-wheelers with motor-cycle engines and tiller steering. Electric cars, so popular at the beginning of the century, still survived to some degree, through improved batteries.

Enthusiastic notice was given to the steam car, 'a delightful car to drive'. It was self-starting, silent, and high-powered, while no great skill was needed in driving as there was no gear-changing. A drawback was that it took five to 15 minutes to get up steam from a cold boiler, and it was damaging to hurry the process. Fuel and water in quantity had to be carried, for the water-tank, especially, needed constant refilling. Except for the containers fixed behind, the 1920 steam car looked like any other car.

Some points on the running costs of petrol cars include the rent of a lock-up garage, from 10 shillings to £1 a week. A motorist could save by not insuring his car, but this was not advised! Depreciation was reckoned at 20 per cent; still, at that period, right after the war, a prewar car would sell second-hand at a much higher figure than it fetched when new. Petrol was about 1s. 6d. a gallon, and a 15 h.p. car did 22 m.p.g. Overall costs for a year's motoring of, say, 9,000 miles worked out at about sevenpence a mile.

Though this was 1920, the *Autocar* contained a passage: 'Very few cars nowadays are fitted with any sprag device.' A sprag was a hinged spike attached to the back axle of the earliest cars. When tackling a steep hill, the motorist let down the sprag to trail on the ground. If the engine stalled and the brakes failed, the sprag would dig into the road and stop the car from running downhill. Evidently some sprags were still extant in 1920.

Before the First World War the motor-cycle was not in great demand. Some interest was aroused by its use in the Isle of Man for the Tourist Trophy races, which began in May 1907. Charles Collier won the first race at $38\frac{1}{2}$ m.p.h., on a 500 c.c. 'Matchless'. A roadster motor-cycle and sidecar combination was in use by 1913, with a four-cylinder, 5 h.p. engine, a gearbox on the rear hub, a chain pedal-starter, and a back-pedalling rear brake. These early machines were excessively long, so that the handlebars extended rearwards with little spread. During the First World War the public imagination was captured by the despatch-rider on his motor-cycle, and after the war supply could not keep up with demand. There were hybrids as well—the bicycle with an engine attached to the back wheel, and the motor-scooter, on which the rider stood holding the handlebars of a glorified child's-scooter machine.

In 1922 Sir Herbert Austin (1886–1941) brought out the famous 'Austin Seven', which, though well designed, did not immediately gain the recognition it deserved. Public opinion needed time to take in the idea of a small car. There were jokes of the type, 'you don't get into it—you just put it on'. Morris did not follow at once; he first modernised the Bullnose to a flat front in 1927, and in 1929 he produced the Morris Minor 7 h.p. smaller car, when the public were used to such a design. At that stage Morris was controlling a great chain of purchased companies, and he was given a baronetcy, which was advanced to a barony five years later. In 1938 he was created Viscount Nuffield.

This extraordinary man was the complete philanthropist; no other public benefactor has given away such vast fortunes. Probably it was his boyhood yearnings that made hospitals the chief target for his boundless generosity; he gave at least £4 million to medical science in one form or another, and about another £4 million to charitable causes. Shares to the value of over £2 million were given in trust for his workpeople. His great fortune was built upon an original capital of £4.

Between 1920 and the early 1930s refinements in car fittings appeared in quick succession. Four-wheel brakes were in use on a few cars early in that period, and as the system spread, a car thus fitted had a red triangle at the back warning drivers behind that it could pull up sharply. There was increased comfort in the independent suspension of wheels, the attention to upholstery and its springs, and the lean-back seating angle. By the end of the period extended seating space had been achieved by carrying the car body out over the rear mudguards, so that the latter no longer stood out from the sides of the car.

Improved lighting and car radio, mechanical windscreen wipers, and swing-out traffic indicators to indicate a turn all combined to improve motoring comfort and standards. Whereas in 1920 an electric starter had merely been one of several starting devices, 10 years later it was standard on all regular cars. In the Daimler Company's fluid flywheel (a flexible hydraulic drive) and automatic gear-change of 1932, there appeared contributions worthy of that great concern.

During the same period there was a marked development in the multi-passenger vehicle known as a 'charabanc' (*83*), which had

83   Charabanc, 1920 and horse-brake, 1907

175

84   Luxury coach, 1968

first been motorised in 1900 by Sidney Straker, of the Daimler Company. Originally this form of transport was styled the 'horse brake', so called because it was fitted with a clog brake for steep hills. When it was mechanised, the old features were retained— long, unpadded seats (hence its French name, meaning 'benched carriage'), open sides, and wooden canopy. In its 1920 form, the charabanc had doors at the ends of each row of padded seats, a fold-back canvas hood, side screens, and solid tyres.

With this long-range and relatively comfortable transport, the country or seaside 'outing' became part of the regular pattern of life. As the popular song ran, 'I do like to be beside the seaside'. Big, roomy omnibuses with two covered decks were in regular use for town services by 1928, so that the noisy and traffic-blocking electric tramcar was on the decline.

On the road itself a number of improvements were being made. Where previously road metal had simply been rolled in, to gather dust which motor traffic threw up in clouds, a primitive tarring system was in use by 1924. Hot tar was sprayed on the surface, and gravel scattered on it stuck to the tar. It was soon developed into 'tarmacadam', a doughy mass of fine gravel and tar, which was rolled upon the road. A defect of 'tarmac' was that it softened, and became sticky under a very hot sun, so the 'dustless' reinforced concrete road was a useful alternative. This was poured in sections, on a wire-mesh base, with a wooden parting-strip between sections. When the concrete was set, the strips were drawn out, and their imprints filled with bitumen. In this way, allowance was made for expansion of the concrete under the weight of traffic.

As the great car-makers struggled for supremacy their efforts put an ever-increasing number of motorists on the road. Under the Ministry of Transport (formed in 1919) carriageways originally designed for horse traffic were expanded and the by-pass road, to skirt congested town centres, was introduced. One useful night-driving device was suggested by a Northcountryman, Percy Shaw. He had noticed that tramlines were a useful guide in foggy weather, and with the backing of the A.A., a reflector system of 'cat's eyes' was laid in the road on the centre line.

Early in the 1930s the winking orange globes known as 'Belisha beacons' (after Hore-Belisha, then Minister of Transport) denoted places where pedestrians should cross the town street. Shortly afterwards, the first experimental 'zebra crossings' appeared—zig-zag white patterns across the road from beacon to beacon. This marking showed a strip of roadway at which drivers must stop if a pedestrian was on the crossing.

An endless variety of traffic travelled the 1930 roads—crowds of Morris Oxfords and Cowleys; Austin, Ford, the fleet of small men's cars. Through them at intervals, silently but for the swish of tyres and lordly brr-umph of warning, swept the stately aristocrats, Rolls, Daimler, Lanchester. On the fringes of the flow, the motor-cycle popped and roared, while the bending cyclist saw it all spin past. It was the beginning of the travelling age, the touring holiday and the weekend jaunt.

In 1930 the Road Traffic Act came as a relief to motorists in general, for they had laboured under an outdated law. Road vehicles were forbidden by the Motor Car Act of 1903 to exceed 20 m.p.h., and this unrealistic limit for 1930 led to much foot-tapping by impatient drivers in fast cars.

Among the rulings of the 1930 Act was third-party insurance, an excellent scheme which covered the motorist against claims. Before this came into force, a person might be crippled for life by a motor-ist who was totally unable to pay compensation; thus the victim could suffer both injury and loss of working time without redress.

Public passenger vehicles were run under licence from special commissioners established by the Road Traffic Act, and a road safety guide called the Highway Code was circulated. This was a booklet of advice and appeal for public cooperation in maintain-ing sensible conduct on the road. However, the steady rise in the accident rate brought a speed limit of 30 m.p.h. in suburban areas.

British motorists were enjoying better roads, better cars, and better servicing, when progress was halted by the Second World War. A drastic cut in petrol for private cars caused thousands of motorists to dig out rusty, neglected bicycles, and to wobble uncertainly down quiet lanes while they recovered the lost art. 'Used cars' and car parts became the centre of a thriving industry; it was not uncommon for a dealer to carry £500 in notes in case he saw a bargain to snap up.

Tyres were at a premium, with retreading a vital service, while synthetic rubber was the subject of intensive experiment. In the tight rationing of petrol by coupon, a check was placed on commercial petrol by dyeing it red, so that any private motorist found with red petrol in his tank would be summoned. There was an undercover service, in which cunning law-evaders bleached red petrol, and sold the result at £1 a gallon. Those motorists who tried tractor vaporising oil found that it ruined the valves.

In view of the great petrol consumption of omnibuses, some economy was needed. A producer-gas plant was devised to burn anthracite that had been treated with soda for reducing clinker, and to improve the performance in making gas, which was fed to the engine. When the latter had been started on petrol, it switched over to gas, doing 70 miles for 320 lbs. of anthracite. It was a nerve-racking system for the driver. He was provided with a handbook of instructions, some of which dealt with situations where he should telephone the depot for instructions on the working of the gas unit.

One of the strangest by-products of the war was that after Germany's defeat the French countryside was littered with

85   Runabout cars: 1910 car and Reliant, 1968

Mercedes cars, abandoned by the Germans through lack of petrol. Some eager Army personnel conveyed cars home, but they found that the Mercedes had been made for wartime military owners, without regard for petrol consumption, and the cars were far too costly to run.

For some years after the war, new cars were in very short supply, so used cars maintained their vital role. It was the summer of 1950 before petrol rationing ceased and there was a steady increase in price. These factors brought a revival of the motorised bicycle, with a light engine driving on the back wheel from the carrier, or some other point of attachment. Another form had the motor built into the front wheel. There was a regular autocycle, with pedals for emergency, and small-wheel motor-scooters were most popular. They were based on the tiny low Corgis issued to parachute troops.

During the 1950s the crippled car industry revived, and the general wage standard led to the biggest upsurge of private motoring that had been seen until then. In the great centres complex schemes were devised to enable the immense volume of mixed traffic to pass through. Main routes were divided with white lines into half-a-dozen lanes; the flyover and the underpass were engineered at right angles to the main route, and the M1 was built, the great north–south motorway, with its high-speed, cruising speed, and slow lanes. On the road, traffic signs grew in number and complexity; light signals for traffic control had been tried in the 1920s, and by 1930 they were in common use. Pedestrians were protected by elaborate 'stop-go' systems installed to direct their crossing, and zebra crossings multiplied.

A holiday-conscious public made great use of the trailer caravan towed behind the car. One disadvantage of the practice was that the engine often became overheated; ordinary cars were not intended for towing. It was better to tow with a Land Rover, or use a regular motorised caravan. Early in the period it was not uncommon to see cycling club members on the road in a large group, but by 1960 this healthy activity had declined. There were two reasons—firstly, the vast increase in motor traffic, and secondly, the exhaust fumes from diesel vehicles.

This period saw the general adoption of the diesel engine for heavy road transport—omnibuses, lorries, and vans. In the diesel, there was a much simpler cycle of operations. No sparking plugs

86   Luxury car of 1968: Rolls-Royce Silver Shadow

were needed, for the spray of heavy-oil vapour was burnt by compression which made it white-hot. Diesel engines were powerful and much cheaper to run than petrol engines, but when they needed servicing they were a great nuisance. Clouds of black smoke came from them, just as from the cars of early motoring days. Though diesel cars were being made before 1960, they never became popular.

In the car industry some new departures had been made which were designed to advance motoring in general. A jet-propelled car, Jet 1, was brought out by the Rover Company in 1950, and some impressive trials were made. This was driving at its simplest, with only brakes and accelerator; there were no gears but reverse, and no clutch. Jet 1 touched 90 m.p.h. on its first trials, while only partly extended.

Such a vehicle was not likely to go into production for a number of years, and the firm's T3 of 1956 was still far from a production model. High fuel consumption had been a great problem, and T3 had brought this down to 12.8 m.p.g. at 80 m.p.h.: the car reached 102 m.p.h. with plenty of reserve power. Both Rover models had rear engines, but Austin produced a front-engine gas-turbine jet in 1955. Another new feature of the Austin car was the heat exchanger, which used the hot waste gases to keep down fuel consumption. In the autumn of 1948 Ford's announced a car jet engine that solved two great problems—the high cost of turbine rotors (several thousand dollars) was reduced to $100, and the heat exchanger was made more efficient.

Even at that date, parking was becoming a gigantic problem. A London experiment to regularise street parking was tested in 1958 as the 'parking meter', a coin-in-the-slot device by which parking space was rented for a set period. This scheme was extended from the original Grosvenor Square region through London's centre during the following year. Suburban street parking was controlled by using yellow lines at the edge of the road, one for limited-period parking, two when parking was prohibited at all times.

At an intersection one might see a roundabout, designed to safeguard traffic following routes at right angles to each other. A driver entering the roundabout from any quarter turned left and went around until he came to his exit turning.

In 1967 Norwich City Council adopted the Continental plan of closing one shopping street to all wheeled vehicles. It led to a 300 per cent increase in the number of pedestrians, and a 25 per cent rise in shop sales. All great towns were concerned with another problem—the derelict cars which were abandoned in thousands every year. Mr Greenwood, Minister of Housing, declared in October 1967 that by 1970 an estimated $1\frac{1}{2}$ million cars per year would go out of use. Disposal methods needed to be on a colossal scale to deal with such masses of scrap metal and useless debris.

There was a revived interest in battery cars during the period 1960–8, and a number of small, light 'shopping cars' were devised by private inventors. A common drawback was the limited range, and in most cases the batteries took at least five hours to charge. Until some kind of compensatory system could be found whereby the car could be run on one battery while the other was being charged, the use of electric cars seemed to be limited. In 1960 there was an attempt in California to trap the sun's energy in a battery of light-sensitive cells, as on a satellite, so that the power could charge the 72-volt battery of a car, but results were not encouraging.

These ideas need further research, but two great features of the 1960s offered considerable advances in motor engineering. One dealt with feed—the fuel injection system, which had been used on Grand Prix racing cars for a number of years. Continental makers of large, costly cars like Mercedes and Lancia had offered the system on their highest-grade models, but Triumph was the first British car to employ it. With fuel injection, there was no carburettor to prepare a mixture of fuel. Instead, it was squirted direct into each cylinder in suitable quantities by means of a metering device. There was completely even distribution, resulting in smoother running with increased power. Of course, the extra efficiency of the injection system meant higher running costs; fuel consumption was estimated at 22 m.p.g.

The second great advance was the Wankel rotary engine (87), a German system of unique principle. A triangular rotor revolved within an oval casing; at the centre of the rotor was a circular hole lined with teeth, and the latter engaged in turn with a fixed gear having two-thirds of this number of teeth (see diagram). There was no cylinder assembly, but as the rotor turned clockwise it compressed a charge of fuel vapour against the wall of the casing. When the charge was fired, by two sparking plugs, it drove the rotor around in the working stroke.

This extraordinary engine, the first serious challenge to the conventional car engine, was on show at Earl's Court in October 1967. It was installed in the German N.S.U. Ro 80 and in the Japanese Mazda Cosmo sports car. Both cars had twin-rotor Wankels, supremely smooth-running at high speeds. N.S.U. Motorenwerken A.G., of Neckersulm, West Germany, had been working on the Wankel since 1960.

Japanese cars and motor-cycles were of remarkably high standard, like all post-1945 Japanese engineering. Production lines and computer-serviced spares depots were super-efficient. Into the British market came Hondas, mini-cars, and motor-cycles, to earn the highest praise from British engineers. German makers were pressing close on Japanese heels with Heinkel bubble-cars and tandem-seat Messerschmitts. All these small models reflected the rising costs, congested traffic routes, and parking difficulties that plagued the British motorist.

In the late 1960s cars have been fitted with a number of safety

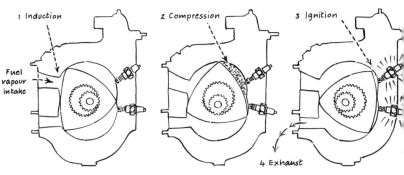

87   Wankel rotary engine

devices—super-efficient power braking, seat belts to prevent the body being thrown forward in a sudden stop, and tubeless tyres, while, in October 1967, stringent tests were introduced for drivers suspected of being under the influence of alcohol. Not all cars were equipped with the compulsory winking turn lights and the regulation stop lights—occasionally a car showed the inadequate swing-out indicator. There was still much progress to be made in the field of safety measures, but, as always, most depended on the motorist.

At the time when cars were still quite common, in 1914, the steam railway locomotive was a sight familiar enough to the British public. Clouds of hissing steam surrounded the engine at rest, when the surplus accumulated on the run-in was released to avoid strain on the boiler.

It was a great thrill to young boys when the metal monster responded to the shrill whistle of the guard by giving a thunderous toot that rang under the arched roof of the station. Next the moving gleam of connecting-rods between cylinders and drivers, moving slowly at first with each bellowing 'chuff'! Sometimes there was the rapture of a dozen rapid chuffs as the monster flexed its muscles and spun its great driving-wheels before beginning in earnest. Chuff—chuff—chuff—chuff—chuff—chuff—chuff, and with billowing smoke above, spurts of foam-white steam below, the shining sleekness drew away, with its retinue of carriages trailing meekly behind.

This was to be the picture for many years to come. By 1920 there existed in Britain 121 railway companies, with small subsidiaries bringing the total to nearly 250, but in the following year all were associated in four great companies. For the north and east of the country there were the London, Midland, and Scottish (7,464 miles of track), with the London and North Eastern (6,464 miles). Southern England and Wales were served by the Great Western (3,765 miles) and the Southern (2,129 miles). In 1933 the London Passenger Transport Board controlled the passenger service in London and district, where all receipts were pooled by the Board and the main-line railway services from outside the city.

Each of the four railway companies had its own special characteristics. Rail and road cooperation was first organised by the G.W.R., with its own delivery service. Until the late 1920s part of the road haulage was done on huge flat drays, drawn by splendid

88　(*Above*) Forerunner of diesel train service: diesel-electric engine 'Deltic', 1955. (*Below*) World champion steam locomotive—'Mallard', 1938

draught horses of great size. These and the big chocolate-and-cream G.W.R. motor lorries were common sights in Western towns. On the railtrack the distinctively coloured passenger coaches made an impressive show, and there was a unique automatic train-control system covering almost all the company's engines.

A great feature of the Southern Railway was its extensive electrified service; by 1939 it had 600 miles on the third-rail principle, the largest coverage of its kind in the world. Another Southern speciality was the automatic coloured signals system.

Though the steam locomotive gained in size and power during the first half of the twentieth century its basic principle remained the same, and the advance in speed was not remarkable. In 1846 Robert Stephenson's long-boiler engines could touch 75 m.p.h. with five coaches, and in 1938 the fastest steam railway engine in the world, 'Mallard', reached 126 m.p.h. between Grantham and Peterborough(88). Mallard, weighing with her tender 126 tons, was the star of the L.N.E.R.; she was a Pacific class 4–6–2 (two pairs of leading wheels, three pairs of coupled driving wheels, and a pair of trailing wheels). In 1964 the famous engine was placed in the Museum of British Transport at Clapham, South-West London. Another high-speed locomotive was on the L.M.A.—the 'Coronation Scot' of 1937, which did a trial run at 114 m.p.h. while drawing a 263-ton train. These engines were streamlined to reduce wind resistance.

A gallant pioneer effort was made at that time to revolutionise rail travel by suspending a carriage on an overhead rail. It was the invention of a Scot, George Bennie, who built his first railplane in 1929 (*89*). Bennie's vehicle was a torpedo-shaped railcar, with an engine and an airscrew at each end, the whole being suspended by spring bogies from an overhead track. Beneath the car, and engaging wheels on it, was a sway-frame of girders to keep the car from swinging. There was a cruising speed of 200 m.p.h., with a peak of 300 m.p.h., braking being applied to the bogies. For an emergency check the airscrews could be reversed.

Fifty seats were provided in the 1929 design, which was successfully run in 1930 above a stretch of the L.N.E.R. line at Milngavie, Stirling. However, the scheme came to nothing, though Mr Bennie was still working on it at the end of the war. An epilogue was provided by a report of the early 1950s which told of the heap of rusting scrap that then represented Bennie's Railplane. Ironically, a monorail service was running with apparent success in Tokyo in 1957.

During the interwar period there was a marked improvement in the comfort and convenience of rail-coaches, with an extension of the corridor type with toilet facilities. Restaurant and sleeping cars were more widely available. An average side-corridor coach was 60 feet long by nine feet wide, and it stood 13 feet high from rail-track to roof. It was divided into seven (first-class) or eight (third-class) compartments, with seats totalling 42 or 64.

There was a competitive spirit between the lines covering the north and south of the country, for they were run as individual

89   George Bennie's Railplane, 1929

companies. Between all four lines, a capital sum of £1,175 million had been expended by 1938. Yet only 10 years later, on 1 January 1948, the companies were nationalised, under the Transport Act of 1947. A new title, British Railways, was applied to the entire network; this became British Rail in the mid-1960s.

All the directors of the former companies were compensated, shareholders received three per cent transport stock, and personnel and rolling stock were taken over in 'regions' by the British Transport Commission. Six regions were arranged—London Midland, Western, Southern, Eastern, North Eastern, and Scottish, with management and operation by the Railway Executive. An immense amount of stock and property was taken over—52,000 miles of track, 20,000 locomotives, 45,000 coaches, 1,230,000 freight wagons, 34,000 motor vehicles, 100 steamships, 50,000 houses, and 70 hotels.

Not many years after this great take-over, diesel locomotives came into prominence, and the decline of steam began. Its disadvantages of coal usage, smoke, and soot on and in the coaches had already brought an expansion of electric train services, and diesels were to strike the final blow. A combination engine was produced by English Electric in 1955—the diesel-electric 'Deltic', 106 tons, which was on trial in October of that year (*88*). It was designed to haul 500 tons at 90 m.p.h. with geared-up speeds to 125 m.p.h.

Diesel engines were one of the main features of the new regime's reorganisation. Until teething troubles were over, there was some difficulty in getting the best out of the new locomotives. One acute embarrassment occurred when the diesel engine of a royal train, which was conveying the Queen, broke down and had to be replaced. There was considerable variety in passenger coaches, a number of a new light type having been made to suit diesel traffic. These coaches were inclined to sway and roll, and they were much overheated. On some provincial lines there were many newly built coaches without corridors or toilets. All the new-style coaches were steel-framed, with sheet-metal bodies; they were stronger than wood, but tended to rattle.

There were ordinary compartment coaches of the traditional kind, and the saloon type with a central vestibule and a partitioned non-smokers' end. In both designs there was usually a toilet at each end. British goods traffic was largely composed of open wagons with tarpaulin covers. It is only in Britain that one finds this great use of the open wagons. All other nations use box-wagons, to be hoisted from carrier to ship by crane. However, most of British trade goes out in shipments, and open wagons are more convenient for crane-loading at the ports.

When they were first brought in diesel locomotives were carefully serviced, so that there were no clouds of black smoke. However, the uncertain future of the railways in later years seemed to be reflected in the condition of the engines. Diesels leaving a station often puffed out evil black smoke in clouds, though they pulled efficiently. By 1965 there was scarcely a steam locomotive to be seen; the last to be built for the British rail-system was taken into service in March 1960. It was 'Evening Star' 2–10–0, a heavy goods engine.

Some alterations in track-laying were tried during the period of change-over from steam. A considerable number of concrete sleepers were laid to replace the time-honoured wooden type. They were effective, but the idea spread much less widely than one would expect. Another completely new venture was seen in 1963— a track-laying train, which put down a hundred yards of steel rail, weighing $4\frac{1}{2}$ tons, in a single welded length.

By 1968 a number of branch lines showed a great falling-off in passenger traffic, owing to increased car ownership. Main-line trains between large centres still bore heavy loads, but numerous closures of provincial branch lines were made, and there was a huge annual loss on the nationalised railway system. A small income from the six privately owned steam locomotives— reckoned at £250,000 a year—was wiped out when, in 1967, British Rail banned them from running on its tracks.

Chapter XIII
SHIPS

B RITISH shipyards had gained so much experience by 1914 that the process of building a ship was an easy, familiar task. Only one yard at the time was completely self-contained; it was a Tyneside firm, the Palmer Shipbuilding and Iron Company. This firm had its own furnaces for ore-smelting, with foundries, steel rolling mills, forges, platers' shops, carpenters' shops, mould lofts, and design departments. A cargo of iron ore could be unloaded at the firm's quay, whence it could be transported to the nearby furnaces. In the ordinary way shipbuilders contracted for their steel, or associated their firms with steel companies.

One of the important preliminaries that shipbuilders carried out was the making of a wax model of the ship's hull for trial. A special centre for experimenting with these models was set up in 1911 as the William Froude Laboratory, part of the National Physical Laboratory, Teddington, Middlesex. In the research centre stood the Alfred Yarrow Tank, 550 feet long, 30 feet wide, and $12\frac{1}{2}$ feet deep. Its windows faced north, in order to exclude bright sunlight which would have softened the wax models, thereby forming a disturbing film on the water and distorting the flow past the model under test.

An overhead 15-ton carriage spanned the tank, with tow lines to the models, and four 40 h.p. motors provided power. Models varied from six to 20 feet long. When the carriage was moving its towing speed ranged from 25 feet per second to 20 feet per minute. At one end of the tank was a motor-driven flap which created the effect of waves, the roughness depending on the flapping speed. In this way the model was going into a head sea, the most trying conditions for a ship. Test-tank information proved invaluable to ship designers—so much so that drawings could be checked for faults in design before a wax model was made, through previous experience. During the testing, the model rose and fell freely while timing, distance, and friction on the hull were recorded by instruments on the carriage. Some self-propelled models, with

90 (*Left*) *Majestic* launched 1913. (*Right*) *Mauretania* launched 1907

electric motors, carried instruments to record the revolutions, torque, and thrust of the screw.

When the Alfred Yarrow Tank had been in use over 20 years, the New Tank was added (1932), with a shallow end to permit water-resistance and steering studies at lesser depth. In the following year Sir James Lithgow of Clydebank provided the money for the Lithgow Propeller Tunnel. It was a large upright structure, like a tube in the form of a hoop, 16 feet in diameter, and with its bore averaging three feet. Here were tested ships' screws in miniature; the models were mounted singly in a chamber in the upper part of the tunnel, and water was circulated to test the screw's efficiency.

This series of careful research activities had not been possible when the most famous ship of the early twentieth century was built, but she was still a fine example of British craftsmanship. *Mauretania*, the great Cunard liner, was built on the Tyne in 1907 by Swan Hunter and Wigham Richardson Ltd (*90*). She was 30,695 tons gross, and for 20 years (1909–29) she held the Blue Riband for the fastest crossing of the Atlantic. On the 1909 voyages she did an average 26·06 knots westward, with 25·89 knots average on the homeward run. Her time from Daunt's Rock, at Cork Harbour Entrance, to Sandy Hook, at New York, was four days, 10 hours, 41 minutes, a record which stood unbeaten for 20 years. With her graceful light hull and red funnels, *Mauretania* was loved by the men of the sea.

Even after she had lost the Riband to the Norddeutscher-Lloyd *Bremen* (27·9 knots) in 1929, the British ship still held her place in

189

the nation's affection. When she was broken up at Rosyth in 1935, her passing was sincerely mourned, though it provided work for thousands of unemployed shipyard men.

Four years after the launching of *Mauretania*, the most tragic ship of that period took the water. *Titanic*, of the White Star Line, was sent on her maiden voyage a year later, on 10 April 1912. She gained more publicity than any ship since the *Great Eastern*. This was the unsinkable ship, at 50,000 tons the largest and the safest that had ever been built. Indeed, she was magnificent; tall and stately, she moved out of Southampton Water *en route* for New York. Four days later she was crossing the iceberg route in the North Atlantic, and moving too fast through that area of deadly danger, *Titanic* struck an iceberg at night. Within two and a half hours she was at the bottom of the sea—a ghastly lesson on over-confidence—and 1,600 people went with her.

This great loss to shipping was a forerunner of the tremendous toll during the First World War. British shipyards were almost deserted at that time, and the destruction of her Merchant Navy made a shipbuilding revival most urgent. A number of German ships were shared out among the Allies as some compensation for losses, so that the great unfinished liner *Bismarck* passed to Britain. She became the White Star *Majestic* (90), one of the largest ships afloat in 1920; her length was 954 feet and her displacement 56,599 tons. Other ex-German ships seized by Britain were *Imperator*, 53,000 tons (renamed *Berengaria* by Cunard), and *Columbus*, which became the White Star *Homeric*.

These ships were not altogether desirable assets, for there had been a good deal of sabotage on board before they were handed over. The constant work and money that had to be expended on them made the ships poor bargains compared with newly built vessels.

Early-twentieth-century ships had been almost entirely run on coal-fired steam engines, but after the First World War there was a general move towards oil-burning ships. This system had many advantages. It cut out the 'black gang'—engine-room stokers—and the mess of coaling, which had the inevitable result of covering the ship with grit.

In firing an oil-burning power plant, a spray of oil fuel was admitted to the burners to produce heat for the boilers. Oil-fuelled ships still used the same form of 'reciprocating' engines, which

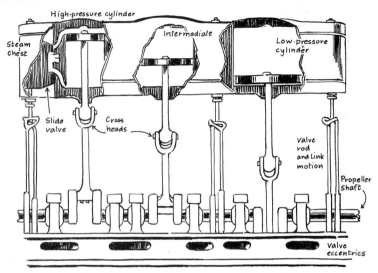

91 Triple-expansion reciprocating engine

were usually of the 'triple expansion' type (*91*). There were three cylinders, normal, large, extra large, with a piston in each. Below the cylinders was a crankshaft like that of a car, with one piston connected to each crank. All three cranks stood at different angles, so that between them they turned the crankshaft completely around as the piston-rods thrust in turn.

When steam was admitted into the upper part of the normal cylinder, it passed through a valve that cut off the flow by a time device. After the expansion of that steam had worked the piston, the same charge of steam was conveyed to the large cylinder next to it, and the steam expanded further to work the second piston. A similar arrangement served the extra large cylinder, where the steam charge was expanded to its last stages before passing to the condenser. This cycle of action by steam admitted into the cylinder above the piston was repeated by a similar cycle below the piston. In that way, each piston was pushed up and down by steam jets in expansion, which explains the term 'reciprocating', i.e. giving back again.

An engine of this type was used to drive a ship's screw (propeller). There was a long propeller-shaft, in three sections, connected with the crankshaft, and the aftermost section extended outside the vessel's stern, with the screw keyed on to it. On the forward

191

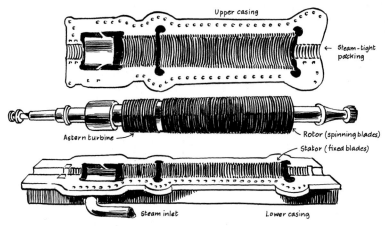

Upper casing

← Steam-tight packing

Astern turbine →

Rotor (spinning blades)

Stator (fixed blades)

Steam inlet

Lower casing

92   Simple turbine unit

section of the shaft, which was coupled to the actual crankshaft, was a stout bracket called the 'thrust block', which took the forward push of the revolving screw.

Oil propulsion of a different kind was used by the diesel engine of the type fitted to many cargo ships after the First World War. This engine was either employed direct upon the propeller-shaft or as a diesel-electric system, where the engine ran generators to produce current for the main engines. Electric drive had a number of advantages, one being the facility of immediate full power in either direction. In the great French liner *Normandie*, launched in 1932(*93*), were electric motors of 160,000 h.p., with current from steam-driven generators.

The steam turbine has a multi-disc rotor, each disc edged with thousands of tiny curved blades(*92*). When the steam enters the turbine casing it is travelling at 75 m.p.h. Having passed between the rotor blades and the fixed blades of the casing or stator, the steam leaves the casing at 600 m.p.h. Turbine rotors spin at such high speeds that the drive is usually through reducing gears to the propeller-shaft. If the screw is turned too fast, 'cavitation' would make it simply thrash a space in the water without giving thrust. For heavy cargo ships the revolutions of the screw can be adjusted by gearing, so that the turbine is spinning perhaps 60 times as fast as the screw.

Main turbines cannot be reversed, so a turbine ship has a small

93   (*Above*) *Queen Mary* launched 1934. (*Below*) *Normandie* launched 1932

'astern turbine', with its rotor blades set contrary to those of the main rotor. Any form of steam engine works more efficiently on superheated steam. Ordinary straight-delivery steam is classed as 'saturated', because it has some water vapour in it, but, if the steam passes over a series of heated tubes on leaving the boiler, it becomes 'dry' or superheated steam, with much more expansion. A Clyde passenger steamer of 1926 was the first ship of any size to use the system—the coal-fired, 20-knot *King George V*, 801 tons.

With these improved propulsive systems, renewed attention was given to the Atlantic speed rivalries. While the French *Normandie*, 80,000 tons, 1,029 feet, was holding the Blue Riband in 1936, a British challenger was in training. *Queen Mary*, of the Cunard-White Star Line, was the peak of British luxury liner building. As No. 534 on Cunard's books, she had suffered a check during her period of building; the economic position in 1931 caused work on her to be suspended for a time. However, she was launched in September 1934—1,019 feet long by 118 feet beam, and when fitted out she displaced 81,237 tons.

It was just two years after Queen Mary had launched the great ship that the Blue Riband was taken from *Normandie*. Britain's finest ship, the largest in the world at that time, averaged 30·57 knots and 30·63 knots on the two-way crossing. After a long period of recovery from industrial depression, it was good for British morale to have the *Queen Mary* (93) at sea. She was oil-fired, with four screws and four turbines and her crew numbered 1,050 men. Such publicity was given her that the tiniest details of her construction were news—10 million rivets and each link of her anchor chain $4\frac{1}{8}$ inches in breadth. Apart from her impressive appearance, she was remarkable in being the first ship of the newly incorporated Cunard-White Star Line, for the two companies had amalgamated in 1934.

In the battle of the Blue Riband *Normandie*, with redesigned screws, regained the coveted trophy in 1937 by a narrow margin. However, by August 1938 *Queen Mary* had taken it again, at 31·69 knots, and it was hers until 1952.

In that year the new American liner *United States*, 51,000 tons, made the crossing in under $3\frac{1}{2}$ days, averaging 35·59 knots—nearly four knots above the British record. *United States* was 990 feet long, and she could take 725 passengers.

No one could have foreseen the ultimate end of *Queen Mary*'s career, or the reason for it. After invaluable service as a troopship during the Second World War, and continued popularity, events of 1966 proved her undoing. In May of that year there was a large-scale strike of merchant seamen, which lasted until July. During that time Cunard suffered a £1$\frac{1}{2}$ million loss of income, and lost a further £1$\frac{1}{2}$ million through the decline of sea passenger traffic. From such losses it was difficult to recover. As a result, *Queen Mary* was put up for sale in the summer of 1967. She was bought by an American, to lie offshore at Long Beach, California, as a floating hotel and entertainment ship. This great liner ended her last transatlantic voyage at Southampton, her home port, on 27 September 1967, before returning to America.

For many years *Queen Mary* had shared the Atlantic run with her sister ship; the latter was launched in 1938 by Queen Elizabeth consort of George VI, and the ship was named after her. While *Queen Elizabeth* was fitting, the outbreak of war changed her role temporarily, and shortly after her maiden voyage in 1940 she became a troopship. This vessel was more massive in form than her sister ship, with two funnels instead of three, and 12 feet longer for her 82,997 tons. Her greater length was due to the housing of an extra anchor in the centre of her bow, creating a more extensive rake. She had berths for 2,262 passengers.

Both the 'Queen' liners were fitted with anti-rolling devices to control movement in heavy seas. This was a serious problem in

94   P. & O. *Canberra*, 1961

big liners, and stabilisers were the accepted remedy. They were first fitted in 1931, to the Italian *Conte di Savoia*, 48,500 tons, 801 feet long, which was built in England. Gyroscopes with massive flywheels were the basic features, and these reduced the roll to three degrees either way. *Queen Elizabeth* was equipped with two sets of Denny-Brown stabilisers in 1955, and three years later her sister ship was similarly treated. A reporter remarked that he had been on board *Queen Mary* when she rolled 25 degrees, causing damage to loose fitments and distress to some passengers. In order to avoid this trouble stabiliser fins were fitted to the ship. They were retractable, and the operation of setting them was carried out with hydraulic rams.

During the 1960s, new trends in shipbuilding brought two particular vessels to the fore. Peninsular and Orient Lines (P. & O.) launched their remarkable *Canberra*, 45,000 tons, $27\frac{1}{2}$ knots on electric motors(*94*). This vessel showed unusual features in the hotel-like design of her superstructure, and the siting of her vents far aft gave a beautiful and elegant sweep towards the bow.

In the case of the other outstanding vessel, a bold step had been taken by America while Britain was hesitating. A nuclear-powered ship was the project on which the British Government contemplated spending £$4\frac{1}{2}$ million. That plan was under discussion early in June 1964; on the 16th of the month the American nuclear ship *Savannah* sailed up the Channel on her maiden voyage. She was powered by superheated steam made through a reactor,

195

95   Oil tanker, *British Admiral*, 1965. 100,000 tons deadweight

in effect an atomic furnace. By means of the continuous chain reaction of splitting uranium nuclei, water was brought to such a heat that it did not vaporise. A circulating pump passed the superheated water through the water in the boiler, reducing it to dry steam, and thence back to the reactor. When the steam had done its work on the turbine, it passed to the condenser, and from that to the boiler as water.

Savannah, 12,220 tons, looked indeed a ship of the future, with her funnel-less superstructure, and the strange form of her three mast-like fitments. She cost £26 million, of which a great deal was expended on the reactor and its shields—six inches each of lead, steel, and plastic. In her reactor was a charge of 690 lbs. of uranium-235, enough for three to four years; the voyage of 3,000 miles from America took about $1\frac{1}{4}$ lbs.

It was admitted that administrative costs were very high, but almost all countries, Britain excluded, provided Government subsidies for their shipping lines as a regular practice at that time. However, it was announced in the autumn of 1967 that *Savannah* would be withdrawn from service, as being uneconomical.

One of the most remarkable things about shipping at that time was the enormous increase in the size of oil tankers. It was due to the effects of the Middle East troubles in 1956. When fighting broke out between Israel and Egypt, British and French forces intervened to keep the combatants away from the Suez Canal. President Nasser blocked the Canal with sunken ships, so that the oil tankers from the Persian Gulf had to sail round the Cape to reach Western Europe. This led tanker owners to build their ships of exceptional size, so that a great cargo of oil could be shipped in one bottom(95). By 1967 the largest tankers displaced well over 140,000 tons.

In that year Cunard saw the launch of a great luxury liner that was the hope of the firm's future. Queen Elizabeth II gave the ship her own name when she sent it down the slipway at John Brown's Clydebank shipyard on 20 September. This new Cunard venture, known while building as Q4, was not as big as the earlier 'Queen' liners. Her displacement was 58,000 tons, her length 963 feet, and her capacity 2,020 passengers.

Cunard made a bold venture in expending many millions on their new ship, though part of her £29 million costs were subsidised by the Government. At that time, transatlantic sea travel was declining very rapidly; in 1957 50 per cent of the Atlantic passengers went by sea, but by 1965 the figure was down to 15 per cent, in the face of keen airways competition.

Queen Elizabeth II(96) was designed as a new-style liner to sail on pleasure cruises with only one-class accommodation—the open-ship plan. For the Atlantic run there were cabin and tourist classes, the basic one-way fare to New York being about £100. It was normal practice to fit a bulbous underwater bow section for better performance, but there were other up-to-the minute features about the new liner. In previous ships, the making of the curved steel plates for the hull was a most important item. These had each a template in wood, with the exact curve required. No

96   *Queen Elizabeth II*, launched in 1967

97 Lifeboat types: (*Above*) *Princess Mary*, Padstow Cornwall. (*Below left*) Inflatable mini-lifeboat for coastal rescue, 1963 (20 knots). (*Below right*) Self-righting boat on trials, 1958 (12 knots)

curved plates were in the new ship's hull. Through skilful design, that expensive process was avoided, though the hull still appeared to be curved as in other vessels. A great deal of weight was saved by using aluminium for the upper works, and vibration was reduced by the fitting of six-bladed screws instead of the normal four-bladed type.

While designers were busy on trade ships and liners, attention was also being given to sea-saviours. Lifeboats(97) had gone through a number of changes since the establishment of the Royal National Lifeboat Institution by Sir William Hillary in 1824. Originally the sailing or rowing boat was taken out to a stricken ship by heartbreaking labour as well as the greatest gallantry. By the early twentieth century, as petrol engines became more reliable, the lifeboat's range was greatly extended, and the crew could devote their energies to rescue rather than rowing.

Three main essentials were required for a lifeboat—strength against heavy seas and rough usage, quick clearance of water taken aboard, and high buoyancy that would keep her afloat after being swamped. Self-righting boats were favoured for some years. This type had endboxes (air chambers) at either end, and there was a heavy keel. However, it was difficult to handle such a boat, so by the 1930s a broad-beamed design was in use, which is almost impossible to overturn.

A good example of a non-turn boat was *Princess Mary*, at Padstow on the North Cornish coast. She was a Barnett-class cabin boat, 61 feet by 15 feet beam, and her twin six-cylinder, 80 h.p. motors could maintain nine knots over a radius of 150 miles. *Princess Mary* had cabin seating for 24 people, and she could take aboard 130 in all. *Sir William Hillary*, at Dover, was specially fitted for air-sea rescue, with twin 375 h.p. engines giving 18 knots—the most powerful lifeboat in the world at that time. Lifeboat engines were carefully equipped with high-level air-pipes and water-excluding insulation. In petrol engines special capsizing switches shut off the engine and the petrol when the boat went over, but there was still the fire risk, so diesels were adopted by about 1933. Among the lifeboat's general equipment were fire-extinguishing jets, a searchlight, radio, a signal lamp, and an oil-spray for rough water.

Though non-turn boats were favoured for so many years, a new type of self-righter was produced at Littlehampton, Sussex, after five years' intensive research by the Lifeboat Institution between 1953 and 1958. A 37-foot, £23,000 boat was built for trials in Osborne's boatyard, and it was deliberately capsized in Littlehampton Harbour in June 1958. After each overturning, the boat righted itself in a few seconds by means of shifting water ballast. On the port side was a 'righting tank' and, when the lifeboat heeled or capsized, $1\frac{1}{2}$ tons of water ballast passed through two square trunks into the righting tanks. This transfer brought her upright again in six seconds, unshipping water. Her twin Perkins diesel engines stopped during the roll, but restarted without trouble.

Five years after the capsizing trials, a mini-lifeboat for the Institution was successfully tested in the same harbour. It was a 16-foot, two-man, inflatable craft, powered by a 44 h.p. outboard motor giving 20 knots. When going into waves 20 feet high, the boat went over at 90 degrees, but its side buoyancy tubes righted it in a few seconds. This little boat was designed for rescue work around the coasts in summer, and it could carry eight survivors.

Chapter XIV

AIRCRAFT

A T a time when British shipbuilders were upholding a great reputation, in 1914 the infant aircraft industry received little encouragement. Aeroplanes did not seem to have any commercial value. Sportsmen and those with a bent for mechanics, such as motorists, were interested in them, but there matters rested.

There were three main centres of English flying—Brooklands, Hendon, and Eastchurch, Isle of Sheppey. At the first two fields flying meetings often took place, and during the period just prior to 1914 a number of important moves were made in England. For instance, Alliott Verdon Roe, of Manchester, founded A. V. Roe & Co., Ltd, and in 1912 produced a design that was a milestone of progress(98). This was the Avro tractor biplane Model 504, whose design was reckoned so satisfactory that it survived almost unaltered until 1928. It was first fitted with an 80 h.p. Gnome rotary engine, in which the cylinders rotated around the central crankshaft, but various other forms of engine were applied later. Another Avro design of 1912 was the first cabin monoplane.

Aircraft of 1914 fell into two categories: 'tractor' designs, where the frontal airscrew pulled the aircraft forward, and 'pushers' with their airscrew behind the engine. Pushers were restricted in design, as the airscrew was arranged centrally between the twin 'longerons' or booms of the girder fuselage. However, it had the advantage that the slipstream (airscrew backwash) was not felt. In the tractor aircraft, pilot and structure received the full force of the slipstream.

Pushers were the choice of the great American air pioneer Samuel Franklin Cody (1862–1913), who became a British subject in 1909. 'Colonel' Cody was a colourful Texan, formerly a circus cowboy, who had experimented with man-lifting kites before he made his name in aircraft. This aviator's great product was his biplane of 43 feet span, which weighed 17 cwt. In Cody's machine, the engine was a six-cylinder Austro-Daimler of 120 h.p.,

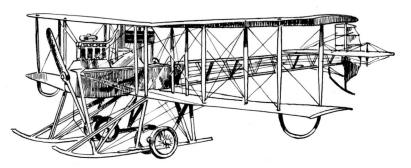

98   Avro tractor biplane, 1911. Prototype of Avro 504

which drove airscrews of the inventor's own design, through reduction gear.

It was Cody who made the first aircraft flight in Britain, at Laffan's Plain, Farnborough, in October 1908, and through skill and daring he became the most prominent aviator in the kingdom. Numerous money prizes fell to him, and they were welcome, for Cody was always short of money through his ambitious ventures.

In September 1912 Cody swept the board at the Salisbury Plain Military Trials, competing against more than 20 machines from different countries. His aircraft was nicknamed the 'Flying Cathedral', supposedly through its great size, but it has been suggested that the word was 'cat-hedral', referring to the down-droop of the wings as opposed to 'dihedral', upswept. Both British and International sections of the trials were victories for the flamboyant airman with his huge pointed moustaches, and he gained £5,000 in prizes. Only a year later Cody was dead amid the wreckage of his beloved machine.

At the time of Cody's death, the establishment of flying schools was an accepted feature. Wilbur Wright had set up the first, at Pau, South-West France, in 1908 and Claude Grahame-White followed suit in 1910. By 1914 the latter was operating a flying school at Hendon, with front-elevator biplanes of his own design. Fees at the school ranged between £75 and £100, and it usually took about two months for a pupil to pass out as proficient.

Among English flyers Louis Blériot's designs were highly regarded, though some of his earlier ones contained some startling features. For instance, Blériot flew in the Rheims International race of 1909, in one of his big monoplanes. On the second lap,

99   Wright engine, 1908

the machine suddenly caught fire and crashed from 100 feet. Though the aircraft was destroyed, Blériot was not badly hurt, except for a good deal of burnt skin. It transpired that he had arranged a temporary rubber tube to carry petrol from the tank to the carburettor! After a short time engine heat caused the tube to perish so that petrol dribbled on the hot exhaust pipe.

Apparently there was a great difference in technique between flying a biplane and a monoplane. In the case of the monoplane, when the motor was out, the nose tended to drop by reason of front engine weight, so the position for gliding in was easily gained. In the pusher biplane, the engine weight was behind the pilot. When forward speed was lost, the tail dropped through rear weight, and the aircraft was likely to sideslip. An experienced biplane pilot would put the nose down before cutting the engine.

'Ailerons' were developed for use on all aircraft. These were hinged flaps at the outer trailing edges of the wings, which were used in banking. On the turning side, the aileron was hinged upwards, to lessen the air hold at that point. At the same time the other aileron was turned down, to give a clawing effect on the air and hold that wing-tip up.

AIRCRAFT

Though crashes were common enough in 1914 they were frequently more damaging to the machine than to the pilot. As the aircraft were of frail construction the wing framework often struck and crumpled before the fuselage containing the pilot so that the initial shock was absorbed. Aviators wore 'retaining belts' as extra safeguard against nose-down crashes, which usually meant the break-up of much framing and fabric before the shock affected the flyers themselves. On occasion when the engine failed a skilled pilot could level off and set his aircraft down like a duck. For instance, if the cut-out occurred above a wood, the aviator would *vol-plane*, as he called it, and at the end of the dive he would pull back his control column to check the speed. This would settle the aircraft in a 'pancake' landing on the tree-tops.

Observers at this time recorded the need for some established evidence on the cause of fatal crashes where there was no clue regarding the tragedy. In those wooden-framed aircraft there was no chance of gauging material fatigue, as can be done with metal. As regards the engine, pilots were advised that, if it missed fire several times, they would do better to seek a safe landing than to fly on hopefully.

In most cases the wooden framework was built of ash and spruce with steel tubing for the undercarriage struts. Throughout the fuselage from end to end ran the main frame members called 'longerons', while spruce 'compression struts' formed the ribs of the fuselage. Between the ribs were lengths of piano wire, drawn taut to brace the whole. When the framework was being covered with fabric (cotton or canvas) waxed twine was used for sewing, or alternatively cane strips fastened with brass screws were fitted. After covering, the fabric was 'doped' with such preparations as 'Raftite', 'Cellon', and 'Emaillite'. Upper surfaces were varnished after doping, to keep off the sunlight, which caused the doped fabric to deteriorate.

In spite of the rapid advances in military aircraft during the years 1914–18, civil aviation gained little. One can see this in the 1916 photographs of instruction aircraft at Grahame-White's Hendon flying school. Students were sent aloft in the old-type front-elevator craft with two open seats. At that date, Grahame-White wrote of the advantages of twin engines, but he did not specify any particular type of aircraft that he had seen using the system.

At the end of the war thousands of aircraft were available, but they were engined for war service when running costs were not considered. There was no immediate promise of a great advance in civil aviation; design and production lagged far behind the work in Germany and America. Defeated Germany, forbidden to make warplanes, concentrated on high-grade transport aircraft and gliders. In America an airmail service covering Washington–Philadelphia–New York had been organised in May 1918.

For Britain, 1919 was the year of advance. In February, the Air Ministry set up a civil aviation department, with multiple duties— licences, Empire air routes, radio services, and weather reports. Shortly after this, on 1 May, came the great step—commercial flying was permitted. It took only two months for the first British airline to be in full operation— Air Transport and Travel Ltd, with a regular service to Paris. It was an obvious move to adapt for civil flying the big multiple-engined aircraft of the wartime bombing squadrons. These also formed the basis of airliner designs.

As heavy, long-range aircraft were ready to hand, there was a natural urge towards long-distance flying, with the Atlantic as the obvious target. After a number of gallant flyers, such as Hawker and Grieve, had been let down by engine failure, the historic flight was accomplished on 14 and 15 June. Captain John Alcock, formerly of the Royal Naval Air Service, piloted a Vickers-Vimy ex-bomber from St John's, Newfoundland, to a landing in an Irish bog at Clifden, Co. Galway. With his navigator, Lieutenant Arthur Whitten-Brown (1886–1948),

100 Captain John Alcock and Lieutenant Arthur Whitten-Brown, 1919

Captain Alcock, then aged 27, flew for 15 hours 57 minutes at an average speed of 118·5 m.p.h. (*100*).

Some slight alterations had been made in the bomber, so that extra fuel could be carried, but otherwise it was of regulation design. In its construction a combination of spruce, three-ply, and steel tubing was covered with fabric, and there was a biplane tail assembly. A big fuel tank was fitted into the nose of the Vickers, with the airmen's seats side by side behind it, and the aircraft was powered by two 360 h.p. Rolls-Royce Eagle VIII engines. When ready for flight, the overall loaded weight was six tons.

It was typical of the developed stamina in aircraft that the ex-bomber, lumbering above the grey, tossing Atlantic, met and shouldered aside the varying weather conditions to be found in a flight of 1,890 miles. These two flyers, borne aloft in a shell of wood and canvas, do not seem to have been unduly perturbed by the perils of the journey, even when, on one occasion, they were upside-down in a fog. With typical Service mentality, Lieutenant Whitten-Brown regularly logged his observations; phlegmatically Captain Alcock weighed up, decided on, and met competently the successive hazards. Neither gales, nor thunder, nor the sight of hungry, bearded, grey waves below could shake the stolid Service calm. Even when the Vickers planted her nose in the Galway bog, and cocked her tail skyward, her antics merited little more than a few laconic words. This was in sharp contrast to the excited chatter of the Irish country folk as they surrounded the stricken monster. Both the intrepid flyers were knighted, but before the year was out Alcock had been killed in a crash near Rouen.

Towards the end of that eventful year of 1919, another great British flight traced an air highway to Australia, between 12 November and 10 December. Captain Ross-Smith, with his navigator Lieutenant Keith Macpherson, performed the feat in a Vickers-Vimy.

During the next few years, airliners were front-page news. Handley Page converted the sword into the ploughshare by stripping down their V/1500 long-range night bomber to fit in 45 passengers and three crew. It could take these people and about five tons of cargo to a range of up to 500 miles. British airlines found their costs high in flying ex-bombers; for that reason the airmail charge on a letter to Paris was 2*s.* 6*d.* and the passenger fare £25. This was a disadvantage, for French airlines enjoyed a

101 (*Above*) Handley Page airliner, Prince Henry, 1922. (*Below*) Bomber
into airliner: Handley Page 0/700, 1919

Government subsidy. As a result two British companies went out
of business in 1921—Aircraft Transport, and Handley Page Ltd.

Frederick Handley Page (knighted 1942) made a great contribution to general safety in 1920, when he was working on his slotted
wing device. This was designed to smooth out the disturbed air at
the trailing edge of the wing, where the air current broke up after
following the under-curve of the wing. Page's slots, sloping from
under-wing to upper, were ranged along the trailing edge, and they
induced air to flow from the upper surface through the slots to
smooth out the eddies under the wing-edge. In this way added lift
was created and maintained, especially when there was danger of
a stall, i.e. a slip back when the climb was too steep for the engine
power.

Flourishing Continental airlines caused four British companies
to unite as a national concern in 1924. Daimler Hire Ltd, Instone
Air Ltd, Handley Page, and Aircraft Transport adopted the
collective title of Imperial Airways. Government funds provided
the capital, and a million-pound subsidy was granted over a period

of 10 years. During that time the airline established a fine record of safe and efficient operation.

About 1925 the old-type rotary engine, with its anti-clockwise spin of the cylinder assembly, was largely replaced by 'radial' engines, whose cylinders were fixed radially around a rotating crankshaft. In-line engines, with the cylinders in rows above the crankshaft, formed with the radial type the two main aircraft power units. Rotary engines had compelled the pilot to bias his steering to starboard, as the spin of the cylinders created a twist to port. Airscrews tended to do the same, so that heavy aircraft were fitted with contra-rotating screws, which evened up the twist. These had been used by the Wrights.

Aircraft design was studied intensively during the period 1920–30. Warplanes had been, at best, an expensive makeshift as airliners, so designers sought a machine of moderate speed and running costs, combined with carrying capacity. One of the most popular ideas was the 'highlift' wing, of thick section, whose design gave less forward speed but took greater load. This aerodynamic form, with well-disposed airflow and lift, had been promoted by Anthony Fokker, the Dutch designer, in 1920. A thick wing allowed the support structure to be self-contained, and dispensed with rigging wires.

Clean design having been established, construction material was considered, and by 1923 metal was an accepted medium. It had been employed in Germany for several years on individual types without exciting great attention. Now the drive on costs revealed that metal was cheaper to maintain than wood, despite the difference in building outlay.

Most countries used duralumin, which was about 94 per cent aluminium with a little copper, manganese, and magnesium, but English builders made up sections of strip steel. Of course, this was more difficult to work, but the builders did not trust light alloys until they had been proved.

In that air-minded age of the mid-1920s Sir Alan Cobham was one of the most prominent figures. His carefully planned long-distance flights were the pathfinders for commercial routes, not bids for fame, and his 'air circus' of large and small machines toured Britain extensively. Public interest was very much increased when the De Havilland Aircraft Company brought out a light machine, the 'Moth' of 1925. It was one of the most popular civil

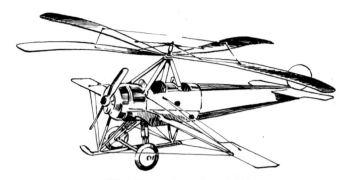

102   Cierva Autogiro of 1926

aircraft ever produced. In fact, at a selling price of £650 the Moth was a remarkable machine. A 27–60 h.p. engine gave it a top speed of 90 m.p.h.; its wingspread measured 29 feet and it weighed about seven hundredweight unloaded. Its unique feature was that the wings folded back on rear hinges, so that the Moth could be housed in any garage giving a space 10 feet wide by nine feet high, with 12 feet from front to rear. It was in a Gipsy Moth that Amy Johnson made her famous solo flight to Australia, and the machine is still preserved in the Science Museum in London.

For many years before the first human flight with wings, designers had dreamed of a rotating-wing aircraft, but it was not until 1923 that a practical design was made public by the inventor, Juan de la Cierva (1895–1936). Cierva's machine, called the 'Auto-giro' (*102*), was built by A. V. Roe & Co. in 1926. Its four-bladed overhead rotor was 30 feet in diameter, and it was started by spinning the rotor with a rope; while the rotor spun, the airscrew ran off the engine. After a short run, the Autogiro took off, supported by the rotating vanes above, and when coming in it landed almost vertically. A number of similar machines followed, but they had names like 'rotaplane'—only Cierva's maintained the name Autogiro. All these craft had the same defect as Cierva's —the rotor was free of the engine, being rotated only by the for-ward flight. In later rotating-wing craft this was not the case.

During the 1930s there was much research and experiment on the twin projects of improved design and engine power. This drew attention to the racing seaplane, an aircraft first devised in a practical form about 1911, as a hydroplane. At that date it was simply a land aircraft with plywood floats instead of skids or wheels, but the principle was developed after the First World War. Famous in this branch of aviation service was the oldest established firm of builders, founded by Eustace and Oswald Short at Rochester, Kent, in 1898. Short flying-boats became a household word, but the Supermarine Aviation Company were responsible for the high-speed seaplane designs. These were the work of Reginald Joseph Mitchell, appointed chief designer of the firm in 1920.

Mitchell's racing aircraft were made prominent by the international air races for the Schneider Trophy, presented by Jacques Schneider in 1913. The first race was won by M. Prevost, at a speed of 45·75 m.p.h. In 1927 a Supermarine-Napier with a 900 h.p. engine weighing only 920 lbs. won the race at just under 282 m.p.h. Two years later an S.6 from the same firm won at $328\frac{1}{2}$ m.p.h., and in 1931 Flight-Lieutenant J. N. Boothman in the S.6B took the trophy outright for Britain at 340·08 m.p.h. Soon afterwards, S.6B, piloted by Flight-Lieutenant Stainforth, set up a world record by covering three kilometres at $407\frac{1}{2}$ m.p.h.

These aircraft were typical of speed designs, with streamlined fuselage and floats: the latter were fuel-tanks, with more in the starboard float to balance the twist of the airscrew turning to port. In S.6B the power unit was a 2,300 h.p. 12-cylinder Rolls-Royce driving a duralumin airscrew.

Some interesting work was done between 1930 and 1940 on the inherently stable aircraft in tailless form. This was pioneered by J. W. Dunne, who built several biplanes of the type between 1906 and 1913. Dunne's biplane wings were swept back so that the *nacelle* (short fuselage) was at the peak of the right angle thus formed, and control surfaces—ailerons and rudders—were at the wingtips. A pusher airscrew was driven by a 60 h.p. Green engine, to give 55 m.p.h. in the 1911 design.

In 1932 a tailless monoplane or 'flying wing', named the 'Pterodactyl', was brought out by the Westland Aircraft Company, on the design of Captain G. T. R. Hill. This machine, first planned in 1926, was swept back 30 degrees, with a pusher airscrew; a small stub-wing was later added at the nose to relieve a slight heaviness. As with Dunne's aircraft, the ailerons were of differential type, to be used together as elevators or separately as ailerons, and small vertical rudders at the wingtips completed the control assembly. It was considered that with the stationary centre o⌐ pressure created by that form of aircraft wing, stalling was almos⌐ completely eliminated. In later years the flying wing was furthe⌐ developed.

A pick-a-back type of airlift was introduced in 1937, in con⌐ nection with the North Atlantic mail route. It was the idea of th⌐ designer, Robert Hobart Mayo, to provide a stepped-up servic⌐ for Imperial Airways. Mayo's composite aircraft consisted of ⌐ giant four-engined Short flying-boat 'Maia' (mother), carrying o⌐ her back a four-engined seaplane, 'Mercury'. With her eight-to⌐ load of mail and petrol, Mercury could not take off independently⌐ so Maia carried her into the air. When the securing tackle wa⌐ released, Mercury flew off alone. This manœuvre was only mad⌐ possible by the stout structure of Maia, with her metal frame an⌐ skin.

A number of wood-and-fabric aircraft were still being made ir⌐ 1940, but the various metal preparations were more reliable⌐ Duralumin was often employed with a covering of pure aluminium⌐ (Alclad), or with rolled-on metal sheeting (Aldural). Wooden air⌐ screws were made by glueing layers of wood together and rough⌐ carving them on an automatic profiling machine. These wer⌐ usually for light sports aircraft, but for heavier duty the airscrew⌐ was stamped or pressed from metal. At that time (1940) experi⌐ ments with plastics were going on; plywood impregnated with⌐ liquid plastic was tried as a fuselage material, and news of a one⌐ piece plastic fuselage came from America.

During the 1939–45 war the petrol-fed piston engine was brough⌐ to its ultimate stage. Speeds of just over 500 m.p.h. were reached⌐ but nothing more could be gained by adding to the banks o⌐ cylinders. A new system was already under development; since⌐ 1937 Frank Whittle of the Royal Air Force had been on specia⌐ duty for his work on jet propulsion. His first test-bed jet engine ran⌐ in that year, and his first jet-powered aircraft, the Gloster-Whittl⌐ E28/39 flew in 1941 (*103*).

In its simplest form this principle was the burning of paraffir⌐ vapour in a chamber that was open at the rear. As the burning⌐ gases expanded in all directions, some found the outlet at the rear⌐ so that the pressure was less in that part of the chamber than ir⌐ any other. By the law of opposites, pressure was highest in the⌐ part furthest removed from the rear, so that expanding gases

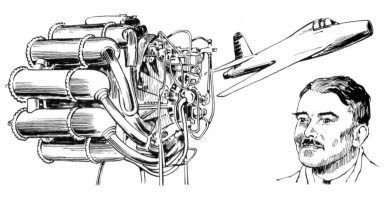

103   (*Left*) Original jet engine W1. (*Above right*) Gloster-Whittle aircraft, 1941. (*Below right*) Sir Frank Whittle at 50

pushing against the front of the chamber produced forward motion.

Usually a turbine was fitted inside the rear of the combustion chamber. It was spun by the hot gases going outwards, and at the forward end of the same shaft was a compressor acting on the air intake at the front. In this way a mixture of compressed air and gas, burning in the chamber, created forward thrust and worked the compressor. When the jet engine was used in heavy-duty aircraft it was best to fit airscrews (these were called turbo-prop engines). As the 'pitch' or twist form of the airscrew blades could be altered while revolving, the blades could be used like variable gears in getting a heavily laden aircraft off the ground. In the same way, a variation of pitch was a form of brake when a loaded aircraft was going in to land.

A simpler form of power unit was the 'ram-jet', a mere tube in which fuel vapour was burnt for thrust. It could only be used to boost another power source, for it had to be travelling at speed before enough air pressure would collect in the tube to mix effectively with the spray of fuel.

Pure-jet engines, without airscrews, were fitted to the most outstanding aircraft of the postwar period, the De Havilland 'Comet' airliner of 1949. It was the first jet airliner in the world to run a regular service, so this brought British civil airways to the front. The Comet cruised at 450 m.p.h. over a 3,000-mile range at six to seven miles high. In the Comet I were fitted four De Havilland

Ghost turbo-jets, and she seated 36 passengers. Later models had more seating, e.g. the Comet II carried 42, having the additional thrust of Rolls-Royce Avon engines. These graceful and popular airliners were the true pioneers of the new air-travel age. As the 'ceiling' was so high, the cabin was pressurised to maintain the normal atmospheric conditions. Elliptical windows were fitted, this being the best shape to bear air-pressure stresses. There was no riveting in the structure: all the metal was bonded, to give a super-smooth outside finish and reduce maintenance.

Just as the Comet was first to be in operation as a pure-jet airliner, the Vickers 'Viscount' became the pioneer prop-jet or turbo-prop of that class. It was a 32-seater, with four Rolls-Royce Dart engines, and the prototype was flown in 1948. At that time, mechanised navigation aids were familiar. An automatic pilot, 'George', had been in regular use since 1938. This was a gyroscope device, that corrected any deviation from the set course. A fully loaded transport aircraft, controlled by radio, was steered across the Atlantic in this way and landed safely. 'George' was the basis of later automatic control devices of remarkable quality.

In that period of jet development, a mighty piston-engine airliner was building at the Bristol Aeroplane Company's factories. This was 'Brabazon I', named after Lord Brabazon of Tara, the first British pilot to gain a certificate. Brabazon I was 177 feet long, with a 230-foot wing span, and it was powered by eight 2,500-h.p. Bristol Proteus engines driving four contra-rotating airscrews. In spite of its impressive size (140 tons), no airline was interested, so after 1950 the huge machine was broken up at a loss of millions of pounds. Another tremendous undertaking of that kind was the Saunders-Roe 'Princess' flying-boat, over 140 tons, with 10 Bristol Proteus turbo-jets. Three Princesses were ordered by the Ministry of Civil Aviation in 1946, but the order was later withdrawn, and the great machines became as redundant as the Brabazon.

A coveted goal for aircraft builders was a contract from the British Overseas Airways Corporation, a public body that had been established under the B.O.A. Act of 1939. It took over Imperial Airways and British Airways in 1940, and under the Civil Aviation Act of 1946 B.O.A.C. became the largest of three corporations that were intended to develop civil airlines.

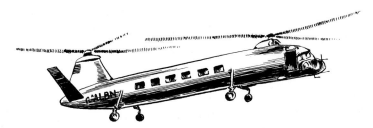

104   Bristol 173: first British twin-rotor helicopter, 1952

In 1952 the Bristol company were building for B.O.A.C. their new 'Britannia', a very successful four-engined prop-jet for carrying up to 104 passengers. Britannia's Bristol Proteus 3 engines, of 4,000 h.p., gave a radius of 5,000 miles and a top speed of 400 m.p.h.

Another postwar development of vast importance was in helicopter design. This was the work of Igor Sikorsky, who devised the power-driven lifting and propelling rotor, which had variable-pitch blades. In taking off, the pitch was increased, so that the blades gave maximum lift. At the top of his climb, the pilot altered the pitch for just enough purchase to hover. When he wished to move forward, a control lever so arranged the blades that as each passed the tail the pitch was increased for a moment, then it returned to normal. By this means, the greatest lift was exerted behind the centre of gravity, so the helicopter was tilted up and moved forward. If the reverse took place, with the greatest lift before the nose of the machine, its tail was depressed and it flew backwards. Steering to port or starboard was effected by Sikorsky's vertical tail rotor, whose pitch was normally set to balance the twist given by the main rotor. Increased or decreased pitch on the tail rotor gave the required steering deviation. In going down, the pilot reduced the main rotor pitch to give less purchase on the air, and the machine sank vertically.

Westland Aircraft of Yeovil, Somerset, did most to bring the helicopter to the fore, with the Westland-Sikorsky S51, in the spring of 1951. Two machines based on that early type, and classed S55, were the first rotating-wing aircraft to fly the Atlantic; they took $4\frac{1}{2}$ hours, in July 1951. Westland built the Sikorsky under American licence. Early in 1952 Britain's first twin-rotor machine was seen as the Bristol 173(*104*). This could take 13 passengers at 142 m.p.h., with its 550 h.p. Alvis Leonides engines. A further

105 Anglo-French 'Concorde', 1968. Supersonic airliner and cabin of 'Concorde'

advance was the Fairey Aviation Company's 'Gyrodyne', a prototype of 1954 which had small ram-jets on the rotor tips—the first British machine of the kind. By 1960 the gas turbine had been applied to the helicopter, and in 1967 a new system was announced to dispense with variable pitch. A gyroscope set over the power unit influenced the steering by its change of position and subsequent correction.

Space will not permit a more detailed study of the various types and their advance in size, speed, power, and scope. During the 1960s, the target was a supersonic airliner to fly in the stratosphere, and work was going on with variable-geometry designs. This implied movable wing surfaces, so that in take-off the full wing area would be used for lift, but in flight the wings would be folded back to half their original size. It is not a new plan. As early as 1916, Claude Grahame-White had written in his *Learning to Fly*: 'In the future, by the use of machines which have the power of increasing or reducing their wing surface while in flight, it should be possible to descend in a space no larger, say, than a garden. . . .'

British and French engineers worked on the 'Concorde' airliner of supersonic speed (*105*) as a combined project and West Germany joined them for a three-way venture—the European 'airbus', to seat nearly 300. These machines had power units whose thrust per pound of fuel was nearly treble that of the original

Whittle engine. His proportion had been 1·5 lbs. of fuel to one pound of thrust, whereas the figure of the 1960s was 0·65 lbs. of fuel to one pound of thrust. Additional thrust was given by the Rolls-Royce after-burner system, by which fuel was sprayed into the exhaust flame, creating a second pressure in the jet-pipe.

One of the problems of supersonic flight is the 'sonic boom', the double report heard when an aircraft 'breaks the sound barrier'. This sound is caused by the piling up of air compression before the nose of an aircraft, and a similar compression in front of the tail. These cone-shaped pressure waves act as funnels, sending earthwards the sharp sounds, caused by the change of pressure as the aircraft's speed outstrips the speed of sound (Mach 1, 760 m.p.h. at sea level, but considerably lower in thinner atmosphere at height). John Derry, test pilot for the De Havilland company, was the first British pilot to exceed the speed of sound, in a DH-108 research aircraft in 1946.

An extraordinary form of flight was made public in 1958, when the Cockerell hovercraft was introduced (*106*). This was the first successful application of the air-cushion system, where a downthrust of air from a piston engine formed a cushion on which a broad, flat hull was borne up. C. S. Cockerell was a boat-builder of Somerleyton, Suffolk. His idea was rapidly developed, so that by 1961 a two-ton Saunders-Roe hovercraft could reach 60–65 knots while skimming a foot or so above the surface.

During the summer of 1966 an experimental hovercraft ferry was run between Southsea and Ryde, Isle of Wight, and the author travelled on the machine. It was a SRN-6, tremendously noisy, with a prop-jet as its propulsive unit. This craft held about 30, and when it was closed up for travel the atmosphere became moist and clammy. Spray prevented any view from the windows, and there was a good deal of judder when the air-cushion passed over the troughs of waves. However, it was a rapid flight—almost exactly five minutes for the five-mile journey.

106 Hovercraft

In this survey our whole concern has been with heavier-than-air flight, but until 1930 many British designers were interested in the dirigible (steerable) airships. All their passenger dirigibles were based on the remarkably successful airship of Count Ferdinand von Zeppelin (1838–1917), which he built as his second effort, in 1908. This was a cigar-shaped gas-container of rubberised cotton, with aluminium boat cars fixed below, and two 110 h.p. Daimler-Mercedes engines. Each of the latter drove two airscrews, one pair forward, one pair aft. There was a rigid frame of aluminium, and partitions of the same metal to divide the 16 gas compartments.

This was a giant vessel, 480 feet long and 48 feet in diameter. She could lift 15 tons, and the top speed was 35 m.p.h. with a favouring wind. At the stern was an assembly of rudders, stabilisers, and dipping planes, the latter being small movable surfaces to lead in the up or down movements. Similar dipping planes were at the bow of the airship, and, as dirigibles were unable to come to earth, they were moored by the nose in hangars.

When a Zeppelin was brought down at Cuffley in 1916 it was in good enough condition to be a useful guide to British airship-builders. A number of good vessels were made, with the serial numbers on R; the airships R33 and R34 were partly finished when the war ended, so they were completed as semi-civilian craft. In view of the progress in airliners there was not much point in producing dirigibles, but this was still going on during the 1920s. A flight in one of these huge, graceful vessels was rather like a sea voyage; the airship rolled and plunged in disturbed conditions, and the relatively low speed exposed it to wind force.

R34(*107*) made the first double crossing of the Atlantic in 1919,

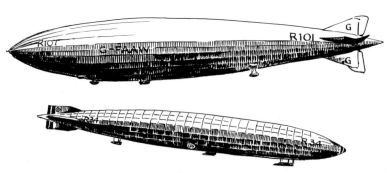

107   R101: Tragic loss, 1930. R34: First double crossing of Atlantic, 1919

with a total of 75 hours' flying time. Another of the series, R38, was bought in 1921 by an American company, though it was a tragic business deal. This was a poorly constructed craft, but in spite of obvious weaknesses, it was kept in service until it broke up in the air with a death-roll of 44. Still the great ships of the sky continued in production until a shock brought the business to an end in 1930, when R101 set out from Cardington, in Bedfordshire. She was on a flight to India, this powerful dirigible with a top speed of 75 m.p.h. and a lift of 73 tons.

On board were the Minister of Air, Lord Thomson, Sir Sefton Brancker, Director of Civil Aviation, and several of Britain's most prominent airship experts. Only a few hours after her departure, R101(*107*) was a huge mass of blazing wreckage on a stretch of open grassland near Beauvais, in Northern France. Six men of the 54 on board escaped with their lives, and the rest, after lying in Westminster Hall, were taken in procession through London for burial in a mass grave at Cardington. Public outcry over the tragedy brought about the dismantling of the sister craft R100, and no further dirigibles were built officially in England. In fact, the last such vessel to be built in the country was the 'Bournemouth' (1951), the private project of a group of enthusiasts to whom the glamour of that man-made floating cloud meant more than its hazards.

BIBLIOGRAPHY

The Home
Barley, M. W., *The House and Home* (Studio Vista, 1963).
Osborne, A. L., *'Country Life' Pocket Guide to English Domestic Architecture* (Country Life, 1967).
Richards, J. M., *Miniature History of the English House* (Architectural Press, 1965).
Richardson, S. and D., *Your Home and You* (Evan Bros., 1965).
Yarwood, D., *The English Home* (Batsford, 1959).

The Kitchen
Ellacott, S. E., ed., *The Story of the Kitchen* (Methuen, 1964).
Smallshaw, K., *Housewife's Book of Home Equipment* (Odhams, 1959).

Family Life and the Advance of Women
Acworth, E., *The New Matriarchy* (Gollancz, 1965).
International Council of Women, *Women in a Changing World* (Routledge, 1966).
Mitchell, D., *Women on the Warpath* (Cape, 1966).
Winnicott, D. W., *The Family and Individual Development* (Tavistock Publications, 1965).
Wynn, M., *Fatherless Families* (Michael Joseph, 1964).

Fashion
British Rayon and Synthetic Fibres Manual (Harlequin Press, 1954).
Ellacott, S. E., ed., *Spinning and Weaving* (Methuen, 1962).
Willett, C., and Cunnington, P., *A Picture History of English Costume* (Studio Vista, 1960).
Williams, N., *Powder and Paint* (Longmans, 1957).
Yarwood, D., *English Costume* (Batsford, 1967).

The Juvenile Revolution
Bailey, L. C., *Youth to the Rescue* (A. James, 1967).
Davis, C., *Room to Grow* (U.L.P., 1967).
Freud, A., *Normality and Pathology in Childhood* (Hogarth Press, 1966).
Goetschius and Tash, *Working with Unattached Youth* (Routledge, 1967).
Ingleby, A. H. B., *Towards Maturity* (Hale, 1966).

Expansion in Education
Bantock, G. H., *Education in an Industrial Society* (Faber, 1963).
Barnard, H. C., ed., *History of English Education* (U.L.P., 1961).
Douglas, J. W. B., *The Home and the School* (McGibbon and Kee, 1964).
Douglas, J. W. B., *Education and the Urban Child* (McGibbon and Kee, 1964).
Jackson, B., and Marsden, D., *Education and the Working Class* (Routledge, 1962).
Musgrove, F., *The Family, Education, and Society* (Routledge, 1966).

The Farm
Addy, J., *The Agrarian Revolution* (Longmans, 1965).
Holmes, G. A., *Revolution in Agriculture* (Todd Publishing Co., 1948).
Laverton, S., *Irrigation* (O.U.P., 1964).
Russell, Sir E. J., *History of Agricultural Science in Great Britain* (Allen and Unwin, 1966).
Street, A. G., *Feather Bedding* (Faber, 1964).
Watson, J., and Moore, J., *Science and Practice of British Farming* (Oliver and Boyd, 1945).

Work and Industry
Davies, A. V., *Science and Practice of Welding* (C.U.P., 1956).
Howard, G. D., ed., *Modern Foundry Practice* (Odhams Press, 1958).
MacMillan, R. H., *Automation* (C.U.P., 1956).
Rolt, L. T. C., *Tools for the Job (a History of Machine Tools)* (Batsford, 1964).
Sharlin, H. I., *The Making of the Electrical Age* (Abelard-Schuman, 1963).
Wright-Baker, ed., *Modern Workshop Technology* (Cleaver-Hume Press, 1960).

Medicine
Carlisle, N. V., and J., *Marvels of Medical Engineering* (Oak Tree Press, 1967).
Cartwright, F. F., *Development of Modern Surgery* (Arthur Baker, 1967).
Hodson, M., *Doctors and Patients* (Hodder, 1967).
Singer and Underwood, *Short History of Medicine* (O.U.P., 1964).
Stevens, R. A., *Medical Practice in Modern England* (Yale University Press, 1966).

The Welfare State
Abrams, M., *Family Needs and Social Services* (Allen and Unwin, 1961).
Beveridge, W. H., *Full Employment in a Free Society* (Allen and Unwin, 1944).
Social Insurance and Allied Services—The Beveridge Report, 1942 (H.M.S.O.).
Goldman, P., *The Welfare State* (Joseph, 1964).
Rooke, P., *The Growth of the Social Services* (Weidenfeld and Nicolson, 1968).
Williams, G., *The Coming of the Welfare State* (Allen and Unwin, 1967).

BIBLIOGRAPHY

Entertainment
   Clunes, A., ed., *The British Theatre* (Cassell, 1964).
   Dowding, G. V., ed., *Book of Practical Television* (Amalgamated Press, 1935).
   Holm, W. A., *Colour Television Explained* (Philips Technical Library, 1963).
   Nicoll, A., ed., *Development of the Theatre* (Harrap, 1959).
   Rotha, P., ed., *The Film Till Now* (Spring Books, 1967).

Road and Rail
   Cornwall, E. L., *Commercial Vehicles* (Batsford, 1963).
   Ellacott, S. E., ed., *Wheels on the Road* (Methuen, 1967).
   Jarman and Barraclough, *The Bullnose Morris* (MacDonald, 1965).
   Loxton, H., *Railways* (Paul Hamlyn, 1964).
   Redmayne, P., *Transport by Land* (Murray, 1948).
   Rolt, L. T. C., *Motoring History* (Studio Vista, 1964).
   Simmons, J., *Transport* (Studio Vista, 1962).

Ships
   Clark, D., *Ships and Seamen* (Longmans, 1950).
   Ellacott, S. E., ed., *The Story of Ships* (Methuen, 1958).
   Harnack, E. P., ed., *All About Ships and Shipping* (Faber, 1959).
   McDowell, W., *The Shape of Ships* (Hutchinson, 1951).
   Phillips-Birt, D., *Ships and Boats* (Studio Vista, 1966).
   Redmayne, P., *Transport by Sea* (Murray, 1950).
   Van Loon, H. W., *Ships* (Harrap, 1935).

Aircraft
   Canby, C., *A History of Flight* (Leisure Arts, 1962).
   Davies, D. P., *Handling the Big Jets* (A.R.B., 1967).
   Desoutter, D. M., *Your Book of Hovercraft* (Faber, 1965).
   Ellacott, S. E., ed., *The Story of Aircraft* (Methuen, 1967).
   Gibbs-Smith, C., *The Aeroplane* (H.M.S.O., 1960).
   Lacey, G. W. B., *Flying Since 1913* (H.M.S.O., 1966).
   Munson, K., *Civil Aircraft of Yesteryear* (Ian Allen, 1967)
   Stewart, O., *Aviation* (Faber, 1966).

INDEX

The numerals in **bold type** *refer to illustration numbers*

220

INDEX

INDEX